ADVANCED WOODWORKING

This volume is part of a series offering home
owners detailed instructions on repairs,
construction and improvements which they can
undertake themselves.

HOME REPAIR
AND IMPROVEMENT

ADVANCED WOODWORKING

BY THE EDITORS OF
TIME-LIFE BOOKS

TIME-LIFE BOOKS
AMSTERDAM

TIME-LIFE BOOKS

EUROPEAN EDITOR: Kit van Tulleken
Assistant European Editor: Gillian Moore
Design Director: Ed Skyner
Chief of Research: Vanessa Kramer
Chief Sub-Editor: Ilse Gray

HOME REPAIR AND IMPROVEMENT

EDITORIAL STAFF FOR ADVANCED WOODWORKING
Editor: Robert M. Jones
Assistant Editors: Betsy Frankel, Brooke Stoddard
Designer: Edward Frank
Picture Editor: Adrian Allen
Text Editors: Robert A. Doyle (senior), Lynn R.
Addison, Peter Pocock
Staff Writers: Patricia C. Bangs, Jan Leslie Cook, Carol
J. Corner, Rachel Cox, Steven J. Forbis, Kathleen M.
Kiely, Victoria W. Monks, Kirk Young Saunders, Ania
Savage, Mary-Sherman Willis
Researcher: Kimberly K. Lewis
Art Associates: George Bell, Fred Holz, Lorraine D.
Rivard, Peter C. Simmons
Editorial Assistant: Susan Larson

EUROPEAN EDITION
Series Director: Jackie Matthews
Text Director: Charles Boyle
Writers: Chris Farman, Fergus Fleming, Martin
Leighton
Researcher: Stephen Jones
Designer: Linda McVinnie
Design Assistants: Andy Monks, Mike Snell
Sub-Editors: Wendy Gibbons, Hilary Hockman

EDITORIAL PRODUCTION
Co-ordinator: Nikki Allen
Assistant: Maureen Kelly
Editorial Department: Theresa John, Debra Lelliott

THE CONSULTANTS: Leslie Stokes was a self-employed carpenter and joiner
for seven years, specializing in purpose-made joinery and internal
fittings. Since 1976 he has taught in the building department at the
Hammersmith and West London College.

Alan Bayliss served his apprenticeship with a leading Sydney cabinet-
making firm and worked as a carpenter and cabinet-maker for 18 years.
Since 1970 he has been a teacher of cabinet-making at Sydney Technical
College.

Roswell W. Ard is a consulting structural engineer and a professional
home inspector. He has written professionally on the structural uses of
wood and on wood-frame construction techniques, and is experienced in
finish carpentry.

Peter Danko, a designer-craftsman, specializes in commissioned
woodworking. A chair of his design received a Daphne Award from the
American Hardwood Institute and is included in the Design Study
Collection of the Museum of Modern Art in New York City.

Lawrence R. England works in the family cabinetmaking and
woodworking business established by his grandfather in Boston in 1900.
The firm specializes in the design and construction of custom-made
furniture.

Stanley N. Wellborn has written many articles on woodworking and
woodworkers. An avid hobbyist, Wellborn specializes in wood-turning
and lathe work, particularly faceplate turning.

Contents

1

Rough Wood to Smooth Boards

For the woodworker who gazes at a tree and envisages a table within its trunk, or who examines rough boards and sees a panelled wall, design must temporarily take second place to the preparation of the stock. Nature does not provide for tables and panels to spring full-blown from the trunks of trees or the surfaces of boards. Much work must be done on the raw material before it is suitable for woodworking. The timber must be cut to size, smoothed to a silky finish and then dimensioned to fit the project in hand.

Wood that is bought from builders' merchants and timber yards—the normal sources of supply for the home woodworker—will usually have been cut to nominal standard sizes; some yards will also custom cut wood to your specifications. But the scarcity and high cost of the hardwoods used in fine woodworking make a search for alternative sources appealing. Some of the best wood used by professional woodworkers is purchased from timber merchants who specialize in high-quality hardwoods; it may also be discovered by reading advertisements in specialist magazines or even by studying notices of estate sales of country properties, which often advertise stores of wood along with the furnishing of homes and farms. Farmers themselves, in the course of clearing land, may fill their sheds with good oak, beech or sycamore logs and then offer them for sale.

The method by which raw—or "green"—wood is sawn into rough stock will determine the grain pattern of the finished boards; in fact, learning to anticipate how growth patterns and grain figurings will react to milling is one of the keys to fine craftsmanship. The wood must then be dried out to reduce its moisture content—a process known as seasoning—before being shaped into boards with straight, parallel faces. Taking time to carry out this work carefully will not only result in a precisely dimensioned board that will ensure smooth joints and easy assembly, but will also disclose valuable information on the nature of the wood—how it grew, how it will respond to shaping, how it can be manipulated. In Scandinavian countries, woodworkers serving their apprenticeships spend up to five years learning to prepare stock and to understand the character of wood before they are allowed to participate in the actual fabrication of a piece.

Just as it is possible for the connoisseur of fine furniture or joinery to appreciate superior workmanship without ever picking up a tool, so it is possible, of course, for a woodworker to love a piece of wood without ever having laid eyes on the original tree. But the process of preparing the wood from scratch, of converting a bark-covered log into smooth boards, can only deepen the woodworker's knowledge and understanding of this unpredictable material, and enhance his pleasure in creating the ultimate design.

Understanding Wood

Wood, one of the world's most ubiquitous natural resources, is also one of the most mysterious. Beautiful to look at and satisfying to work, wood often seems to have a life of its own. For one thing, it has a disconcerting tendency to continue to react to the atmosphere long after it has been cut, surfaced and finished.

Fortunately, it is well within the power of the woodworker to control and manipulate this tendency, and doing so is one of the charms of the craft. By understanding how wood grows and what happens to it as it dries, the woodworker can anticipate and influence its behaviour. He can, for example, pre-shrink the wood by seasoning it, modify the design of the piece to allow for potential shrinking and swelling, or finish the piece to control its response to the environment.

The most commonly used terms in describing wood are probably "hardwood" and "softwood". Hardwoods, the kind most often used for fine woodworking, come from broad-leaved deciduous trees and are, indeed, generally hard. Softwoods come from needle-leaved evergreen trees, or conifers, and are generally soft. However, the wood of some deciduous trees, such as balsa, is actually soft, while the wood of some conifers, such as yew, is hard.

The characteristics of wood are also determined by the structure of the tree; certain qualities are associated with certain parts. Heartwood, the older wood at the centre of the trunk, is often valued for its moisture resistance, for example, while the younger sapwood is more responsive to moisture variations.

How the tree grows will determine the figuring of the wood—that is, the natural colouring patterns and texture of the grain—which, in turn, affects the way the wood will finish. Coarse-grained woods, such as oak and ash, have large, open cells which, when cut, produce a slightly pitted surface. Fine-grained woods, such as maple and birch, have small, thick-walled cells, producing a smooth surface.

The pattern of the grain on a milled board is largely a reflection of the growth rings, but it can be emphasized or softened by the manner in which the log is cut. When timber is sliced across the rings at a sharp angle, as in quarter-sawing *(page 10)*, its graining, or figure, will be linear. On the other hand, plain-sawing *(page 10)*, in which the cuts are roughly parallel to the concentric rings, will tend to provide an arced grain.

After the primary conversion from log to rough-cut board, the timber must then be seasoned, or dried, until its moisture content is in the correct range *(page 12)*. At this stage, many problems can occur that affect the behaviour of the timber when it reaches the woodworker's hands. Imperfect drying can result in warping *(page 13)*, checking *(page 10)* or case hardening. In case hardening, the outside of the wood dries more rapidly than the inside, and interior splitting called honeycombing occurs. There are two sure methods by which you can avoid such problems: either buy kiln-dried timber, or air-dry green timber yourself at home under carefully controlled conditions *(page 12)*.

When you buy softwood, whether green or kiln-dried, remember that it is graded according to clarity, or freedom from blemishes. Most softwoods are imported, and the system of grading varies from country to country. Timber merchants in Britain generally sort their wood into three grades: prime joinery, standard joinery and building grade or carcassing.

Prime joinery is expensive, so it is worth using only when the wood is to be given a particularly good finish—with stain or polish, for example. Standard joinery is normally used for trimmings, such as architraves and skirtings, and carcassing quality timber for work where appearance is unimportant. You may come across other grading systems—if so, ask the timber merchant to explain them. Although hardwoods are not usually graded, you should be able to find less than perfect boards at a reduced price.

Hints on Buying Timber

Whenever possible, purchase your timber where you can make your own selection, and choose with these points in mind:

□ Avoid boards with dead knots *(overleaf)*. They weaken the timber, often become loose and can fall out.

□ Be wary of boards which are warped, bowed, cupped or twisted *(page 13)*, as it may be impossible to correct the defect. Look along the length of each board before buying, to see that it is as straight as possible. A badly warped length is most often the result of poor seasoning, and it can create serious problems when you come to use it.

□ Watch out for boards with cracks or splits *(overleaf)*. If these occur near the ends of the boards, you can simply cut them away. However, if they are very long, getting rid of them can reduce the effective length of a board.

□ Look out for boards that still have bark on the edges. Getting rid of these so-called waney edges can reduce the effective width of a board.

□ Examine the growth rings on the end of the timber *(below)*, and avoid boards where they are widely spaced. Such boards are likely to be weak.

□ Avoid boards which feel particularly heavy—this could be a sign that they have not been properly dried and still contain too much moisture.

□ If you are buying planed timber, make sure that the machining is up to standard. Poor machining leaves the surface with a distinct ripple running across the width. It can also result in surfaces which are not parallel or square.

Flaws in the Tree That Affect the Timber

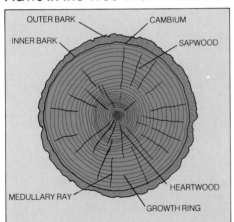

Anatomy of an average tree. The usable wood in the trunk of a tree lies beneath a protective layer of outer bark, or cortex, and two thin layers of life-supporting tissue. One of these thin layers, the inner bark, also known as the bast or phloem, carries food from the leaves to the rest of the tree. The other, the cell-producing cambium, is where the cell growth for both the wood and the outer bark takes place.

The first layer of usable wood, nearest the cambium, is the light-coloured sapwood, which carries sap from the roots to the leaves—a function that makes it liable to attack from fungi and insects. The heartwood, beneath the sapwood, is denser and darker and generally more durable; it contains resins, for instance, that make it more resistant to rot. Most of the concentric growth rings represent one year of life, and each is composed of a layer of light springwood and one of darker summerwood, reflecting the two seasons of growth. A high proportion of summerwood to springwood results in a richer, darker coloured wood. Radiating from the heart, or medulla, are the medullary rays, which carry food laterally and sometimes produce a pronounced pattern in the milled timber.

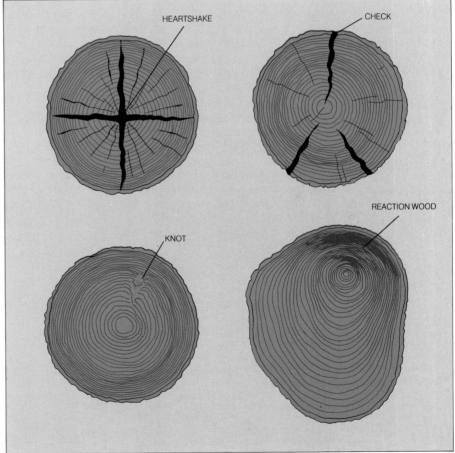

A record of assaults. Most trees are subjected at some point in their lives to conditions that alter their normal development and leave behind defects and injuries. Heartshake, a result of decay or stress, forces a tree to crack at the centre and to split along the medullary rays. Checks, which are generally less severe, appear as splits or cracks after the tree is felled. These are caused by separation of wood fibres along the grain and across the growth rings as a result of uneven shrinking. Knots are the ends of broken limbs that have subsequently become encased by new growth. Reaction wood, identifiable by its off-centre pattern of growth rings, is found in trees that lean sideways because of high winds or a one-directional light source.

Characteristics Created During the Milling Process

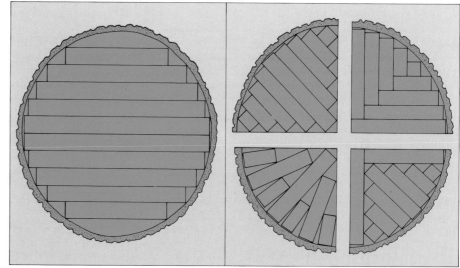

Variations in milling techniques. In plain-sawing *(near right)*, the simplest and most common method, the log is sliced lengthways, or tangentially, into parallel slabs of uniform thickness. This method leaves very little waste, but the boards warp as they dry. In quarter-sawing *(far right)*, the log is cut into quarters, then into slabs. Shown clockwise from lower left are four cutting patterns: a true radial; a modified radial, in which only the centre board runs to the heart; alternating tangential cuts; and a combination of radial and tangential cuts. The true radial is the most desirable. It produces more waste, but it exposes a more attractive grain and yields boards less likely to warp.

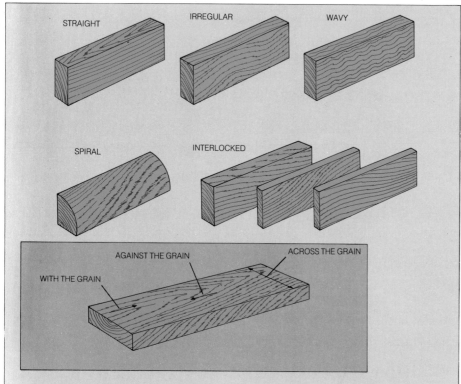

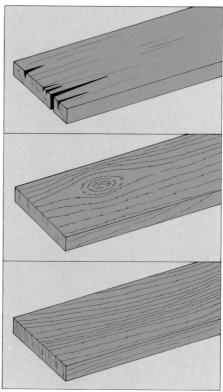

Identifying grain types. Of the five naturally occurring types of grain, straight grain—found in such woods as ash and oak—has the greatest overall strength but produces the least interesting pattern when sawn. Irregular grain is straight grain that has been deflected from its course by a defect, such as a knot; it can be present in almost any wood. Wavy grain is less strong than straight grain but produces attractive patterns; it is found typically in European walnut and sometimes in ash. Spiral grain, often found in chestnut, is grain that follows a corkscrew course up the trunk of the tree, producing diagonal patterns when sawn. Interlocked grain,

shown here with several slices taken from a block of wood to expose its change of direction, follows one course and then another. This erratic grain pattern is commonly found in hardwoods such as African mahogany and sapele.

In addition to forming distinctive patterns, grain also moves in a specific direction, reflecting the tree's upward growth. To find the grain direction on a board *(inset)*, run a plane lightly over its surface. If you are going with the grain, the plane will travel more smoothly; if you are going against the grain, the wood will start to tear. You can also determine grain direction from the way the grain on the edge of the board slants.

Recognizing defects. In the milling process, abnormal growth reappears in the form of defects that may weaken the wood. Checks *(top)* show up as deep cracks in the end of the board or as surface splits; they tend to worsen as the board shrinks and swells. Knots *(centre)* appear as dark whorls, varying in diameter from less than 10 mm to more than 40 mm. If the knot is encased in dead bark, it may eventually loosen and fall out. Reaction wood *(bottom)*, with its compressed rings, shows up as a dark streak in the grain pattern of the board; the tension of the rings may cause the board to be brittle and to shrink unevenly.

A Woodworker's Guide

Material	Characteristics
SOFTWOODS Douglas fir	Medium-fine texture; excellent strength, good bending qualities; good workability; good with nails, screws, glue; excellent finishing qualities (tends to show grain); commonly used for furniture, interior joinery, telegraph poles, ship masts, plywood.
Larch	Coarse to medium texture; excellent strength, fair bending qualities; good workability; difficult with nails, good with screws and glue; good finishing qualities; commonly used for carcassing, garden furniture, exterior joinery.
Parana pine	Fine, even texture; good strength, fair bending qualities; good workability; difficult with nails, good with screws and glue; good finishing qualities; commonly used for interior joinery.
Redwood	Fine texture; good strength and bending qualities; good workability (tends to be knotty); good with nails, screws, glue; good finishing qualities; commonly used for furniture, interior joinery, cladding, plywood.
Western hemlock	Medium-fine texture; good strength and bending qualities; fair workability; good with nails, screws, glue; good finishing qualities; commonly used for carcassing, exterior joinery, plywood.
Western red cedar	Coarse texture; fair strength, very good bending qualities; good workability; fair with nails and screws, good with glue; good finishing qualities; commonly used for exterior joinery.
HARDWOODS Ash	Coarse texture; good strength, excellent bending qualities; good workability; fair with nails, screws, glue; excellent finishing qualities; commonly used for furniture, interior joinery, turning.
Beech	Fine, even texture; excellent strength and bending qualities; fair workability (tends to bind when sawn or drilled); fair with nails, screws, good with glue; good finishing qualities; commonly used for furniture, interior joinery, turning.
Elm	Medium texture; excellent strength and bending qualities; fair workability; fair with nails and screws, good with glue; good finishing qualities; commonly used for furniture, veneer, interior joinery, turning, barge and boat-building.
African mahogany	Medium texture; good strength, fair bending qualities; fair workability; good with nails and screws, glue; excellent finishing qualities; commonly used for furniture, interior joinery, panelling, veneer, turning.
Oak	Coarse texture; excellent strength, good bending qualities; good workability; good with nails, screws, glue; good finishing qualities; commonly used for furniture, veneer, interior joinery.
African walnut	Medium texture; fair strength, good bending qualities; good workability; good with nails, screws, glue; excellent finishing qualities; commonly used for furniture, veneer, interior joinery.

Rating woodworking properties. When logs are converted into boards, the wood acquires characteristics that affect its use and handling. The chart above lists six softwoods and six hardwoods commonly chosen for woodworking projects and describes how they look and behave. Also included is a sampling of their traditional uses.

The term "texture" here applies to the appearance of the grain, not to its tactile qualities. "Strength" and "bending qualities" refer to ability to withstand impact and to bend without splitting. "Workability" describes how the wood responds to tooling. Each wood is also rated for its ability to hold fasteners and glue and to take finishes, such as stain or paint.

The Significance of Seasoning

When a living tree is cut down, more than half its weight may be water. This water is contained as free liquid in the cell cavities and bound liquid in the cell walls. As the tree is converted into boards, the water begins to evaporate; when the free water has gone and the bound water begins to leave, the wood reaches what is known as fibre-saturation point. The moisture content is then between 23 and 35 per cent, depending on the type of wood.

It is not until the moisture content falls below the fibre-saturation point that the wood begins to shrink—a process that continues until the proportion of moisture in the wood is the same as that in the air around it. The wood is then said to have reached an equilibrium moisture content, and it is considered seasoned and ready to be worked.

The fastest way to season wood is to dry it in kilns, or huge ovens, in which steam is used to keep the humidity high while the temperature is kept low. Gradually, the temperature is raised and the humidity is lowered until the moisture content of the wood has been brought down to the desired level. Indeed, where the level needs to be below 20 per cent—as in the case of timber that will be used for furniture and internal joinery—kiln-drying is essential.

Air-drying, a much slower process which takes place out of doors in open-sided sheds and relies on the ambient heat of the sun, can be used for timber customarily dried to a moisture level above 20 per cent—for example, timber used in constructing gates, fencing and garden furniture. Temperature, humidity and air circulation must be strictly controlled so that the boards dry fast enough to prevent the growth of mould but slowly enough to prevent checking. To dry boards to their normal equilibrium moisture content of 20 to 23 per cent takes approximately one year per 25 mm thickness for hardwoods, and slightly less for softwoods.

Begin the air-drying process by marking each board with a number and the date on which the drying commences. Then stack the boards out of doors, but protected from rain and the direct heat of the sun. (If you dry the timber indoors—in a garage or conservatory, for example—cover it with plastic sheeting to prevent it from drying too rapidly, and check it frequently for fungi; if fungi appear, increase air circulation by loosening or removing the plastic and restacking the timber.)

Stack the boards on a firm, level base of concrete or creosoted timber, separating the layers with "stickers"—lengths of 25 by 25 mm timber placed 450 mm apart along the length of the stack and aligned vertically from layer to layer. Place boards of uniform length in each stack; overhanging boards will dry too rapidly and warp. End grain dries almost 12 times as fast as side grain, so coat the ends of the boards generously with PVA glue, aluminium paint or polyurethane varnish to prevent them from splitting.

The moisture content of kiln-dried timber can be calculated by weighing sample boards before and after drying and employing a simple mathematical formula: initial weight less dry weight over dry weight, multiplied by 100. The wood must be dried in the kiln until it stops losing weight.

A more precise, though more expensive method of monitoring moisture content is to use a battery-operated moisture meter. Usually calibrated to cover a range from six to 30 per cent, such a meter determines moisture content by measuring the electrical resistance between two pin-type electrodes that are driven into the wood (opposite page, below).

Bear in mind that, even when timber is seasoned, it will still gain or lose moisture if it is moved between environments with different humidities. Thus boards which have been stored in the open will lose moisture and shrink when brought indoors, particularly into a centrally heated room. It is important, therefore, to allow time for the timber to reach an equilibrium moisture content consistent with its new surroundings. This process, which is known as "second seasoning", may be as little as a few days for small pieces, but well over a week for larger ones.

How Timber Responds to the Drying Process

A predictable pattern of shrinkage. Cuts of timber, superimposed in their original positions on a log, show how wood tends to shrink unevenly as it dries, causing variations in shape. The greatest change occurs in a tangential cut which closely parallels the direction of the growth rings. A radial cut, at right angles to the rings, shrinks half as much. Uneven shrinkage across and along the grain of the rings causes circular cuts to dry to ovals, and square cuts to diamonds.

Changes in shape. When timber dries too rapidly, the normal pattern of shrinkage is exaggerated and the board warps. Although considered defective to some degree, warped boards can often be salvaged by planing or, in more extreme cases by steaming and redrying. The most common kinds of warping are cupping, springing, bowing and twisting. In cupping, the board curves into a hollow across the grain; in springing, the board lies flat but bends along the edges like a hockey stick; in bowing, the board arches from one end to the other; in twisting (also referred to as winding), the board lies flat at one end but cups or springs at the other end.

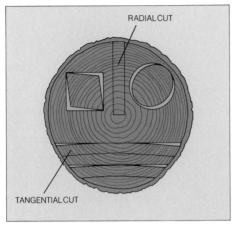

RADIAL CUT

TANGENTIAL CUT

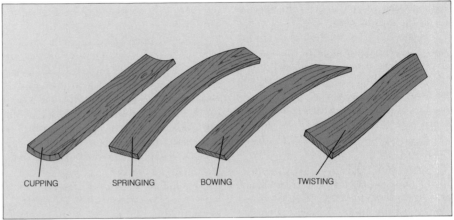

CUPPING SPRINGING BOWING TWISTING

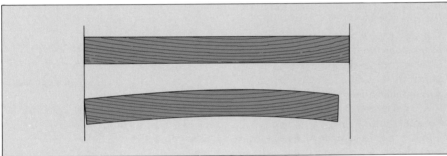

Changes in dimension. Having reached fibre-saturation point, timber behaves rather like a sponge, shrinking as it loses moisture and swelling as it gains moisture. In the upper drawing on the left, a tangentially cut board has been dried to 16 per cent moisture content, a standard amount for stock timber; in the lower drawing, the same board, dried to 10 per cent moisture content for cabinetry and woodworking, has shrunk in width and has also begun to cup. The direction in which a board cups is always opposite to that of the growth rings: the side nearest the centre of the tree becomes convex, the side opposite concave.

A Probe for Measuring Moisture Content

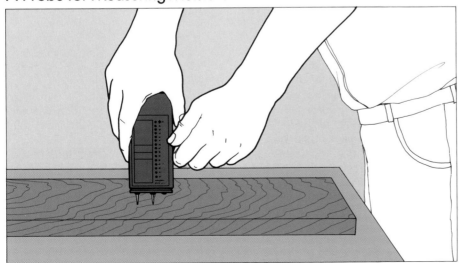

Using a moisture meter. Remove the cap of the meter to expose the light-operated switch. Plunge the sharp metal pins into the timber and note the figure marked on the meter body adjacent to the light that shines. Probe at several points along the board—avoid the ends of the board and the areas around knots, which give up moisture quickly—then average the readings. If testing a board thicker than 75 mm, probe on both face surfaces and along the edges.

Making the Most of Power Tools

Electric drills, routers and other common power tools have a place in most home workshops. Many of the techniques demonstrated in this book, however, involve the use of more specialized—and expensive—tools that may not be familiar.

Some of these tools, such as the combined planer/thicknesser *(page 26)*, are designed for specific purposes; others, such as the spindle moulder *(page 39)*, have more varied applications. When deciding which new tools to buy, always consider your actual needs: a spindle moulder, for example, is useful if you plan to shape complex moulded profiles for architraves or skirtings or to cut a large number of tongue and groove joints, but for a few simple rebates a router is quite adequate. The serious woodworker may alternatively wish to invest in a combination machine *(opposite page)*.

No matter how you eventually decide to equip your workshop, always bear in mind that power tools must be treated with the respect that is due to any piece of potentially dangerous machinery. Follow the specific safety rules for individual power tools every time, and observe the general precautions listed below. When you begin to become familiar with the operation of your new machines, do not be tempted to take short cuts as you work and so increase the risk of injury.

Safety also lies in an efficient and well planned workshop. Lack of space not only hampers the flow of work but can quite easily lead to accidents, especially if two people are using the workshop at the same time, or if you are working sequentially from machine to machine.

Before equipping a workshop, draw a scale plan of the available space and mark in the positions of the equipment you plan to include, arranging pieces in the sequence in which they will be used. Remember to allow space round the machines for working with long lengths of timber or wide panels. Never try to cram an extra machine into a room where there is not the space to use it safely. If possible, position the cutting and shaping tools near the storage area, to avoid the need for carrying large boards across the path of other machines. Similarly, the finishing operations should be carried out near the door of the workshop, so that finished projects can be stored away from the working area.

Keep the floor free of obstructions to permit easy passage between work stations. Choose a flooring that is even, durable and skidproof. Concrete or vinyl are both suitable, but vinyl has the disadvantage that it can become slippery when covered in sawdust. If you have a concrete floor and are using the workshop for long periods of time, position timber duckboards around your machines to provide a more comfortable flooring surface.

Each machine position should be well lit and the whole working area adequately heated—cold fingers fumbling in gloomy conditions can easily lead to accidents. If you plan to do a large amount of work on a regular basis it may be worthwhile investing in a mobile vacuum system on castors. Not only is dust a distracting irritant in a workshop, but large accumulations of sawdust heaped up on the floor can represent a serious and unnecessary fire hazard.

Safety Rules for Power Tools

Safety rules for individual machines are listed on the pages on which the machines are introduced. The following precautions apply to all power tools, and you should ensure that they are known to every person who uses the workshop.

☐ Never operate a power tool when you are tired or ill or have been drinking alcohol or taking medicine.

☐ Keep the work area and tool surface uncluttered and well lit.

☐ Keep the tool clean and lubricated, the blade sharp; check the electrical cable and plug frequently for fraying, nicks or other damage. Make sure the socket and the plug are properly earthed.

☐ Always switch off and unplug the tool before making any adjustments.

☐ Do not wear clothing or jewellery that could catch in moving parts. Keep shirt sleeves buttoned or rolled up. Tuck long hair inside a cap.

☐ Wear safety glasses and, if the operation is dusty, a dust mask.

☐ If you are using a noisy machine in a confined space for lengthy periods, always wear ear protectors.

☐ Feed wood carefully into the blade; never force it to move at a faster rate than the tool can easily accommodate.

☐ Never mark the wood for a saw cut after the motor has been started.

☐ Whenever possible, use the safety aids, such as blade guards and hold-down devices, provided with the tool. If an operation cannot be performed without removing the safety devices, work with extreme caution and, when appropriate, use improvised guards and hold-downs.

☐ After turning a machine off, wait for it to stop completely before touching it.

☐ If a piece of timber jams in a machine and causes it to stall, turn the machine off before attempting to free the timber.

☐ Never leave a power tool running while it is unattended.

☐ Always fully tighten a new blade or bit in its mounting, to avoid damage to the machine or yourself.

☐ Never reach over a turning blade; walk round the machine.

☐ Keep children and pets away from the work area, and keep the room locked when not in use.

☐ Do not let your mind wander; concentrate on what you are doing.

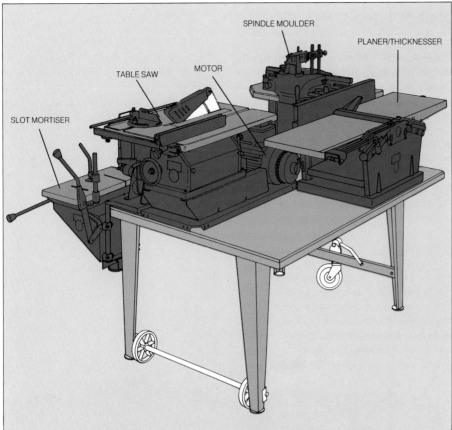

SPINDLE MOULDER

PLANER/THICKNESSER

TABLE SAW   MOTOR

SLOT MORTISER

Multi-purpose combination machines. The two combination machines shown here both take up little space in the workshop and are capable of carrying out a number of woodworking tasks. The more simple model *(left, above)* is designed as a series of individual machines, which allows you to add to the basic unit according to your needs. The machines—here, a table saw, planer/thicknesser, spindle moulder and slot mortiser—are mounted on a sturdy worktable measuring 1300 by 900 mm. The table saw and the enclosed motor on its base plate can be removed from the table and used separately. When mounted on the table, the motor's drive belt can be slipped on to any of the other components. A band saw, sander and grinder, and other compatible machines can be added later to the worktable and powered by the same motor, which can be adjusted for different operating speeds.

The second, more complex machine *(left, below)* combines the functions of a table saw, planer/thicknesser, spindle moulder and slot mortiser in a single compact unit about a metre square. The machine is powered by three motors, and incorporates a sliding table, adjustable fences for the table saw and planer, and a tilting spindle. This machine is much more expensive than the first, but can be adjusted for different jobs more quickly and has many built-in features for the specialist woodworker

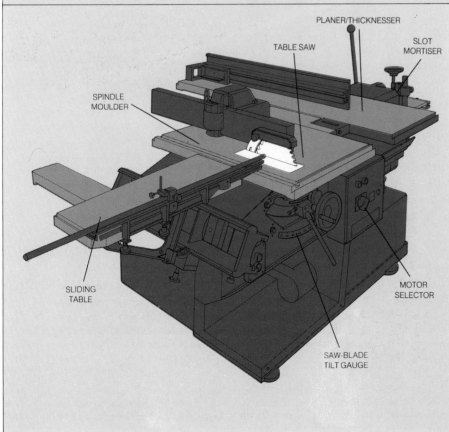

PLANER/THICKNESSER

TABLE SAW

SLOT MORTISER

SPINDLE MOULDER

SLIDING TABLE

MOTOR SELECTOR

SAW-BLADE TILT GAUGE

Cutting Wood to Rough Length and Width

The first step in any woodworking project is to cut the wood roughly to the dimensions required for surfacing, shaping or joining. The initial cuts will also produce boards with straight edges and eliminate many defects that could cause you problems at a later stage.

Whether you are working with milled boards from a timber yard, or chunks cut from logs, a table saw, the basic large machine in a woodworking shop, is the best tool for cutting boards to width (by ripping) and length (by crosscutting). A typical home model, with a blade 225 mm in diameter, can cut through boards up to 75 mm thick. Two saw accessories, the rip fence and the mitre gauge, enable you to cut milled timber to precise widths and angles, and an easily made plywood jig (*opposite page*) will hold irregularly shaped pieces of wood in position for cutting straight edges.

You can get the best results with a table saw if you use the correct blade for the job in hand. A table saw commonly has a combination blade, which can be used for either ripping or crosscutting. However, a blade ground specifically for one job will give a smoother cut on that job. You can improve the performance of any blade by cleaning it periodically with a resin solvent such as turpentine, to prevent binding.

Vibrations from normal use can cause small alignment errors in the adjustable parts of a table saw. The tilt of the blade and the angle of the mitre gauge should be reset at the beginning of each project, as described on the right.

On some table saws, you may need to check periodically the alignment of the saw table with the blade. To do this, unplug the saw, raise the blade fully and mark one tooth with a crayon. Then rotate the blade by hand so that the marked tooth is even with the table surface at the front of the blade slot. Measure from that tooth to each mitre-gauge channel. Then rotate the blade until the marked tooth is at the back of the slot, and measure again. If the front and back measurements are not identical, adjust the table top in accordance with the manufacturer's instructions—usually by loosening the bolts connecting the table to the base, tapping the table top with a rubber mallet until the alignment is perfect, then tightening the bolts.

Use a similar technique to align the rip fence before each ripping job. Position the fence so that the distance from the fence to both the front and the back edges of the saw blade is exactly the width of the planned cut. (Measure to the inner point of a saw tooth closest to the fence.) Lock the fence in place.

Careful selection and careful cutting will enable you to use wood economically. For example, if you are sawing an irregular piece that tapers from one end to the other, you will get the most from it by cutting off the edges; you can then cut wider boards from the broader parts of the piece. You should also be careful to plan your cuts in such a way as to eliminate knots, cracks or other defects in the wood.

When you are sawing around problem areas, extreme caution is necessary. Knock out any loose knots before sawing, to prevent them being thrown by the blade. Sawing through cracks can cause a wedge of wood to pop out with great force.

Aligning the Saw for Precision Cuts

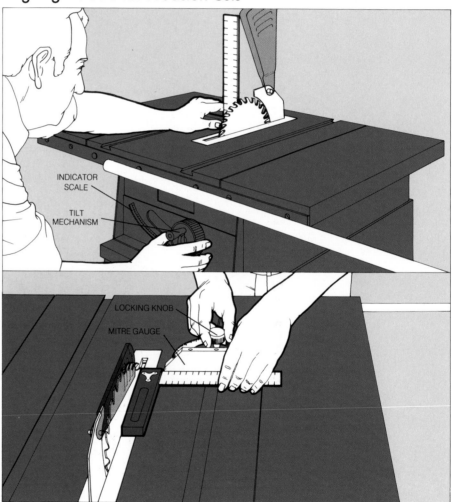

Adjusting the blade and mitre gauge. To check the vertical alignment of the blade *(top)*, unplug the saw, extend the blade fully and set a try square on the table, its tongue vertical against the blade. Use the saw's tilt mechanism to bring the blade flush against the square. If the blade does not move easily, check the track of the tilt mechanism for obstructions. When the blade is perpendicular to the table, adjust the pointer to 0 degrees on the tilt mechanism's indicator scale. For a 90-degree angle on the mitre gauge *(bottom)*, hold a try square's tongue against the mitre gauge and its handle against the saw blade. Pivot the gauge to bring the square's handle flush against the blade, then tighten the locking knob.

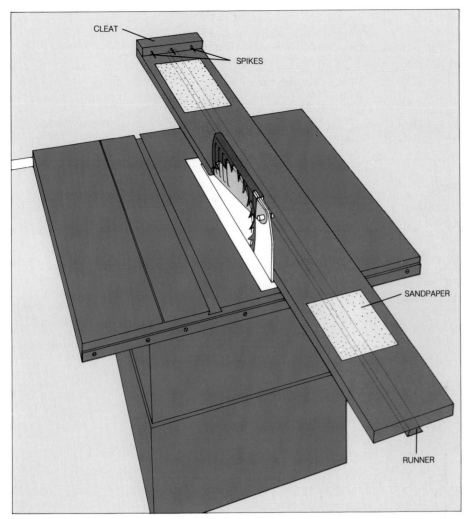

CLEAT
SPIKES
SANDPAPER
RUNNER

A Jig for an Irregular Board

A ripping jig. A long, narrow jig is used to ripcut a straight edge on one side of an irregularly shaped piece of wood; this straight edge can then be held against the rip fence when you are cutting the opposite edge of the board *(page 18)*. The 1.2 metre-long plywood base of the jig is guided by a single hardwood runner that fits into the dovetailed mitre-gauge channel to the left of the saw blade. The runner is positioned so that the right-hand edge of the jig's base is up against the edge of the blade; the runner is attached with countersunk wood screws. A 50 mm-high plywood cleat, used to hold the rough timber in place on the jig, is screwed to the back end of the base, perpendicular to the runner. The pointed ends of nails driven through the cleat and two pieces of coarse sandpaper glued to the top of the base help keep the rough board from shifting as it is sawn.

Guidelines for the Safe Use of a Table Saw

Before you operate a table saw, familiarize yourself with the rules for power tools *(page 14)*. Be sure to follow these specific safety guidelines for the saw:

☐ Keep the surface of the saw clean and free of wood scraps and tools. Keep the working area around the saw clear and well lit.

☐ Use a push stick whenever you are ripping narrow stock. The stick is placed on the stock between the blade and the fence and is used to push the stock completely past the blade.

☐ Stand off to one side of the path of the saw blade.

☐ Hold the wood firmly against the fence or the mitre gauge while cutting. Avoid awkward hand positions that will be hard to hold during the cut.

☐ Provide support at the sides or end of the table when cutting large stock.

☐ Do not remove the blade guard unless you are using a jig that cannot be moved through the guard; replace the guard immediately after making the cut.

☐ Before crosscutting, remove the rip fence from the saw table.

☐ Do not begin a cut until the blade has reached full speed; do not remove the stock until the blade has come to a complete stop.

☐ Never attempt to saw boards freehand; always work using the rip fence, the mitre gauge or a jig.

☐ Do not try to force a stalled blade while the motor is running; if the blade stalls, turn off the saw immediately.

☐ Never reach over the blade.

Straight Edges for a Rough Board

1 Ripping the first rough edge. Place the ripping jig *(page 17)* on the saw table and lay the board on the jig with one end butted against the cleat and the other end just in front of the blade. Then turn on the saw and carefully push the jig across the table, using one hand to press the board down against the jig's base.

2 Ripping the second edge. Position the rip fence to guide the cut, then put the board on the saw table with the newly cut edge against the fence and one end just in front of the blade. Turn on the saw and slowly push the board into the blade with your right hand, initially pressing the board against the fence with your left. When your hands approach the blade guard, push the board with a piece of scrap wood or a push stick held between the saw blade and the fence.

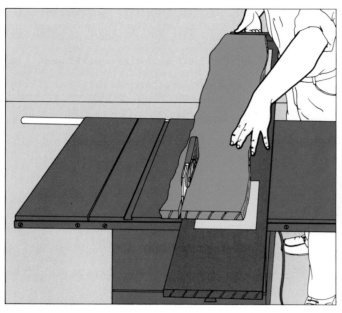

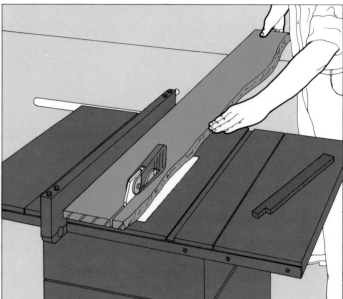

Cutting Square Ends

Crosscutting with the mitre gauge. To prevent long boards from wobbling as they are cut, screw a timber extension to the mitre gauge. Lock the mitre gauge in position at 90 degrees, and adjust the blade height to cut a few millimetres more than the thickness of the board. Butt the board against the mitre gauge extension, align the cutting line on the board with the blade, and switch on the saw. Holding the board against the mitre gauge extension with your left hand, push it towards and past the blade with your right. Keep both hands well away from the blade.

To crosscut several pieces the same length from one board, clamp a timber stop to the table against the rip fence at the front of the saw, the desired distance from the blade *(inset)*. Slide the board up to the stop, then make the cut. Turn off the saw, remove the cut piece, and repeat.

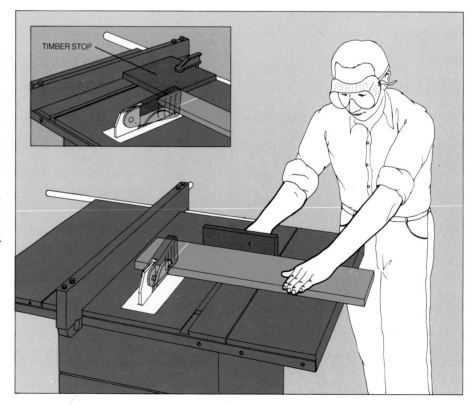

TIMBER STOP

Thin Boards from Thick Ones

A thick length of rough stock can be resawn into two or more thinner boards to suit your requirements. Resawing also allows you to make two pieces of timber that have mirror-image grain patterns, or to cut thin slices for use as inlays.

Although it is possible to resaw wood with a table saw or even a handsaw, the best tool for this job is the band saw. Most band saws designed for home use will cut wood up to about 150 mm thick; because the blade is thin, a minimum of wood is lost as sawdust. Most home band saws have a high blade speed—about 1,000 metres per minute—which is excellent for resawing. A skip-tooth blade, so called because it has widely spaced teeth, is best for this fast cutting. Select the widest blade the saw will accommodate; a blade at least 10 mm wide will facilitate straight sawing.

After installing a new blade—and then periodically while you use the saw—check the blade's tension; a loose blade will not cut smoothly. To check the tension, run the saw briefly to seat the blade on the wheels, then switch off and unplug the motor and open the upper-wheel door. With a finger, push the blade sideways. If there is a deflection of more than 6 mm, use the tension knob to adjust the upper wheel so that the blade is tightened.

Because the flexible blade of the band saw tends to travel along the grain of the wood, you will need to control the timber carefully as you cut. Precise cuts can be made using the adapted fence, illustrated on page 20, to guide the board as it is fed past the blade.

Before you begin to cut, make sure that one edge and one face of the stock are square and straight, so that they bear accurately against the saw table and the fence. The faces that you cut will be left rough by the saw blade, and must be planed smooth to their final dimensions.

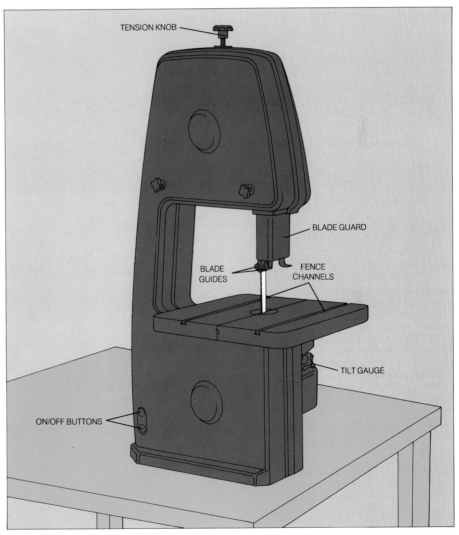

TENSION KNOB

BLADE GUARD

BLADE GUIDES

FENCE CHANNELS

TILT GAUGE

ON/OFF BUTTONS

The versatile band saw. Because it makes a wide range of cuts, from resawing thick stock to cutting delicate curves in thin strips, the band saw is a valuable woodworking asset. Both benchtop models *(above)* and free-standing band saws mounted on wheels are available. The throat (between the blade and the arm) varies from 250 to 350 mm wide; the maximum amount of blade exposed is usually 100 to 170 mm.

The blade is a flexible steel loop that passes around two large wheels. The lower wheel is connected to a motor; the upper wheel, adjustable by a tension knob, turns freely to guide the blade and keep it taut. The table can be tilted up to 45 degrees, and most models have channels for a mitre gauge and a fence.

Setting Up a Band Saw for Precision Cuts

Adjusting the table and the blade. To check that the blade is properly aligned with the table, hold the handle of a try square against the side of the blade so that its tongue is flush against the table. Correct the table alignment if necessary.

With the adjusting screw, set the blade-support bearing *(inset)* so that it does not quite touch the stationary blade, but will revolve immediately pressure is applied to the blade as sawing starts. Turn the blade-guide adjusting screws to bring the guides into position against the sides of the blade, then loosen these guides until you can slip a piece of paper between each guide and the blade. Inspect the blade from its side to be sure that the blade teeth, pointing downwards, are visible in front of the guides.

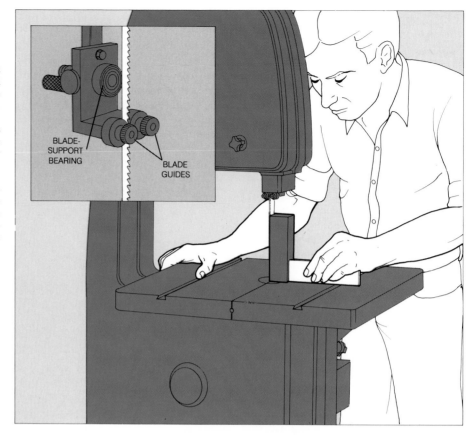

BLADE-SUPPORT BEARING

BLADE GUIDES

How to Resaw a Board

1 **Setting up for the cut.** Slot the parallel fence into its slot on the saw table. Secure a piece of scrap timber the same width as the rough stock to the fence with countersunk screws or, if the fence already has a timber facing, with nails *(right)*. Scribe a pencil line on the top edge of the stock to mark the thickness desired. Set the stock on edge on the table against the fence board, and adjust the fence so that the mark on the board lines up with the teeth on the blade. Then set the blade guides no more than 3 mm higher than the top edge of the stock.

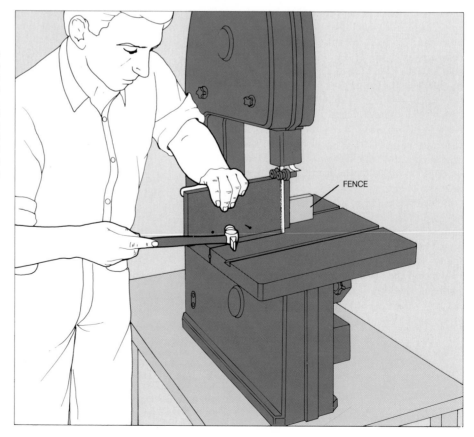

FENCE

2 Starting the cut. With the stock clear of the blade, switch on the saw. Then begin pushing the stock forwards with your right hand so that the blade enters it on the cutting line. Hold your left hand over the fence board and use your fingers to steady the stock against the fence as the stock is fed through. Keep your left hand at the near end of the fence, well back from the blade.

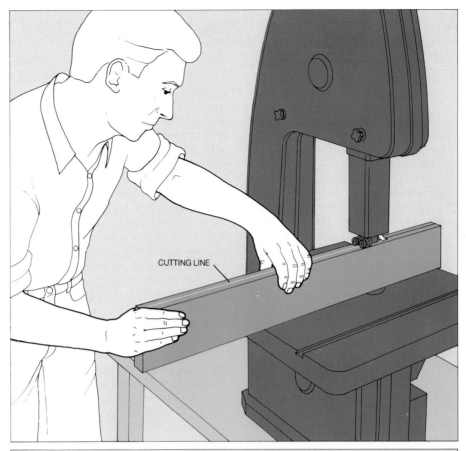

CUTTING LINE

3 Finishing the cut. As you near the end of the cut, use a notched push stick to guide the stock through. Move your left hand to the other side of the blade and support the cut section of the stock against the fence.

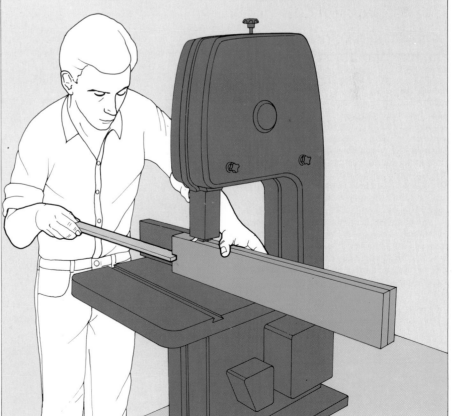

Mirror-Smooth Surfaces Cut with Hand Planes

Once boards have been sawn roughly to size, they will require planing to achieve a smooth finish and exact dimensions. Precise work is called for, because any errors you make at this stage can result in a poor appearance or ill-fitting joints in the finished work. A power planer *(page 26)* is fast and accurate, but not essential. You can achieve mirror-smooth, perfectly flat surfaces on almost any piece of rough wood with nothing more than good-quality hand planes. The same tools also make it possible to make straight, true boards out of twisted or warped wood.

Modern bench planes are precision tools, each designed for a specific purpose. A jack plane, 350 mm long, can be used for smoothing most rough timber. The 500 to 600 mm body of a jointer plane, or trying plane, makes it especially suitable for surfacing boards longer than 600 mm, since it prevents the plane from following the original surface contours of the board. The small block plane, a one-handed tool only 150 mm long, is for planing the ends of boards; its blade is set at a low angle to cut the end grain with a slicing action.

Any board being planed must be firmly secured to your work surface. When planing edges and ends, a vice or clamps are sufficient. For planing the faces of boards, stops against which you can push the workpiece are needed. Workbenches often have holes for bench stops—wooden or plastic pegs that project above the work surface. Or you can improvise stops by nailing strips of plywood to the work surface.

The work surface must be perfectly flat and level. If your bench is uneven, cover it with 12 or 18 mm chipboard or plywood, using wooden shims below it as needed.

Hand planing can be perfected only with practice. To avoid problems that develop if you plane against the grain of a surface or an edge, begin with a test. Set the plane blade for a shallow cut and make a few strokes in each direction. Work in the direction that gives the smoother cut. When you plane a long surface, stand beside the workbench with your outer foot braced in front of you and your shoulders and hips parallel to the plane. To avoid rounding off the corners, control the pressure you apply to the plane throughout the stroke. As you

begin a stroke, press down on the front of the plane; press evenly as you plane along the board, and press down on the rear as you finish the stroke.

Keep the blade, or iron, well sharpened and correctly adjusted. As you work, check and adjust the blade frequently to make sure it is removing a minimum amount of wood. And as you adjust the blade, sighting down the length of the plane's sole from the toe, check the angle of the blade as well as its depth; use the lateral adjusting lever on top of the tool to keep the blade edge exactly parallel with the mouth. Clean the sole with paraffin and lubricate it with candle wax or linseed oil. Always stand the plane on its side to protect the blade.

Using a hand plane to reduce boards to exact dimensions requires careful control. Begin by sawing or planing the board to within 3 mm of its final dimensions. Plane one face until it is perfectly flat and smooth, then one edge until it is straight and square to this first face. Mark these as your face side and face edge, and from them establish reference lines to plane the second edge and second face.

Establishing a Reference: Planing for a Smooth Face

1 **Planing the face.** Place a rough board on the bench with one end butted against a bench stop. If the board is cupped, place it concave face down to prevent it rocking as you work. If it is twisted, place wooden shims beneath it to make it stable. Adjust a jack plane for the first cuts and begin planing off the high spots—in this case the central section. Plane diagonally across the grain *(left inset)*. Then plane at right angles to the first cuts, to eliminate any remaining ridges *(centre inset)*. Having planed away the high spots, adjust the blade for thinner shavings and plane the entire face. Check the board frequently for twisting and flatness *(Steps 2 and 3, opposite)*. For a final smoothing, hold the plane at a slight angle to the grain and move it in a direction parallel to the grain *(right inset)*.

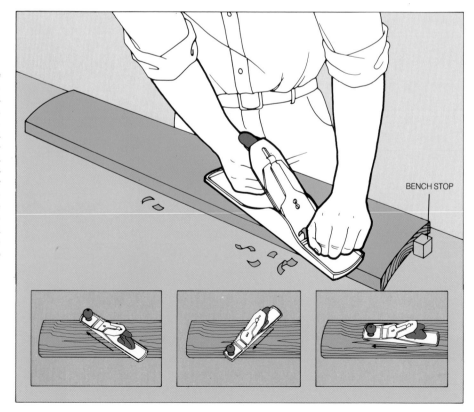

BENCH STOP

2 **Checking for twisting.** Sight down the board with the aid of a pair of winding sticks—straight hardwood battens stood on edge on the face of the board at right angles to the board's edge. Any twisting or winding will show as you sight across the tops of the sticks: the top edges will not be parallel to one another. Move the sticks into different positions to check for twisting along the entire length. Plane down the high spots.

To make the winding sticks, cut two 300 mm lengths of 30 by 6 mm, check that the top and bottom edges are exactly parallel, and chamfer one top edge of each stick *(inset)*. Two steel rules can be used as a substitute for winding sticks, but they are less convenient because they cannot be stood on edge.

CHAMFERED EDGE

3 **Checking for flatness.** Hold a straightedge rule on edge along the length of the board parallel to the edges. With your eyes almost at the level of the board, slide the straightedge towards you. At low spots, light will show through between the straightedge and the board. Check along the entire length of the board. Plane down the high spots and recheck.

Planing the First Edge

1 **Creating a face edge.** Select one edge to become the face edge or reference edge. Clamp the board in the vice with this edge up and the planed face towards you. Adjust the plane blade for the initial cuts and plane the edge, keeping the plane centred and square with the edge by placing your thumb on the toe of the plane and using your knuckles as a guide along the smooth face of the board. Hold the plane so that its sole is parallel to the workbench and the plane is parallel or at a slight angle to the edge of the board. Continue to plane until the edge is flat and square to the face side, checking as you proceed *(Step 2, below)*.

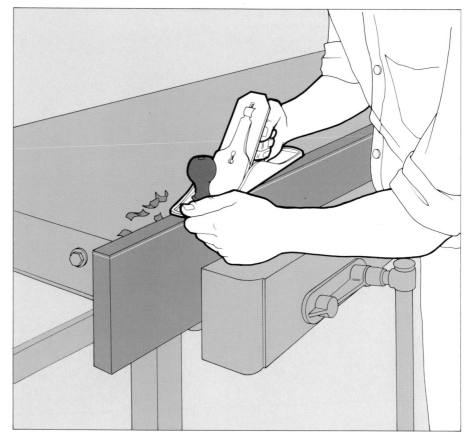

2 **Testing for squareness and flatness.** As you plane the first edge, stop regularly to check that the edge is square to the planed face side, and flat along its length. Hold the board up to the light if possible and, with the stock of a combination square or a try square against the face side, slide the square down the length of the edge, looking for gaps. Hold a straightedge along the length of the edge to look for hollows. Mark any areas that are not square or flat. Return the board to the vice and continue planing, always using the shallowest possible blade setting, and being especially careful to keep the plane level at the areas that are marked.

If one side of the edge is higher than the other, move the plane across towards that side, controlling its position with your free hand, and then continue to plane. The plane will remove shavings from that side of the edge only. Keep the plane parallel to the length of the board, with the sole at right angles to the face side; avoid tilting the plane over to one side.

Squaring the Board

1 **Marking the width.** With the board flat on the workbench, face side up, extend the ruler of a combination square to the desired final width of the board. Place the stock of the square against the planed long edge—the face edge. Hold a pencil vertically at the end of the ruler, and slide the combination square and the pencil down the length of the board in one motion, marking a line that is parallel to the face edge. Repeat on the other side of the board. Using these reference lines, plane the second edge in the same way as the first, checking carefully for squareness.

If the board is less than 200 mm wide, a marking gauge can be used instead of a combination square to mark the reference line.

2 **Marking the thickness.** Clamp the board in a vice and set a marking gauge to the desired thickness on one edge of the board. Hold the stock of the gauge firmly against the face side and pull the gauge along the edge to scribe the line. Begin by marking with gentle pressure on the spur to keep it from wandering; then re-mark the line two or three times with increasing pressure. Do the same on the other edge and both ends. Plane the second face as you did the first *(page 22)*, starting at the high points. As you approach the final thickness, a feathering of the grain at the edges will indicate that you have reached the top of the marking-gauge line. Proceed cautiously, taking care not to cut below the line.

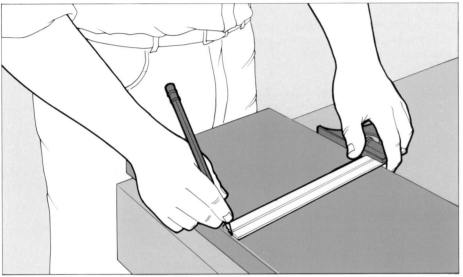
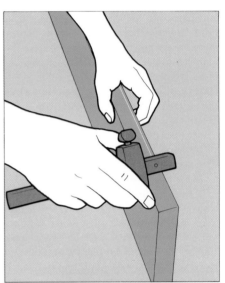

3 **Planing the end grain.** Using a try square or a combination square, and a marking knife or a sharp pencil, mark one end of the board with reference lines at right angles to the long edges. If the board is not too long, clamp it upright in the vice and plane the marked end; clamp longer boards flat on the workbench, with the marked end overhanging the bench edge by 100 mm or so *(right)*. Set a block plane for a shallow cut; plane at a slight angle across the grain, using short, even strokes. To prevent chipping, plane from one edge to the middle; then turn the board over in the clamps and plane from the other edge to the middle. Check for squareness following the instructions given in Step 2, opposite.

Once the end is square, make very shallow cuts across the entire end to smooth and finish. Mark the opposite end of the board with reference lines at the final length of the board, and then plane it in the same manner.

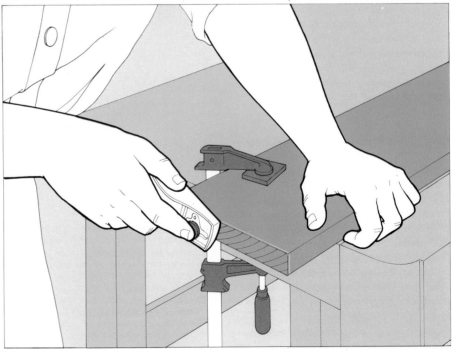

Smoothing with a Power Planer

For fast and accurate smoothing and trimming of timber, two types of motor-driven planer are essential: a surface planer and a thicknesser. A surface planer is used to plane one face of the timber and an adjoining edge so that they are straight and square. A thicknesser is used both to get the second face and edge of the timber parallel with the first, and also to "thickness" a board down to the exact dimensions that you require.

You can save money and space by buying a planer and thicknesser incorporated into one machine, as shown here. Its cutter head, a revolving cylinder with two or more barely protruding blades, divides the planer into two tables. When surface planing a rough board, the infeed table is adjusted for the depth of cut required, while the outfeed table is set at exactly the same height as the top of the blades. Thus, when a board is fed from the infeed table over the cutter head, it is trimmed by the blades and then supported in its diminished thickness by the higher outfeed table (right, inset).

To ensure the most precise planing, the blades should cut with the grain of the wood, and the timber must be fed towards the cutter head at a slow but even pace. Hardwoods should be planed at a slower speed than softwoods. On the model which is illustrated here, the maximum depth of cut is 3 mm.

In addition to planing faces, edges and ends of boards—the three basic jobs described on the following pages—the planer can be used to cut slanting bevels or chamfers along the edge of a board. For this, you adjust the guide fence to the required angle.

To convert the dual-function machine from a planer into a thicknesser, simply swing the planing tables into a vertical position and place a clip-on guard over the cutter head (opposite page, above). Lay the board on the thicknessing table, adjust the height of the table to give the required cutting depth, and select the feed rate; when the machine is switched on, the board is carried automatically past the cutter head by two spring-loaded rollers.

Because the thicknessing table is underneath the cutter head, the timber is fed through the thicknesser in the opposite direction to that in which it is planed (opposite page, above, inset). The cutter will re-

move no more than 3 mm; to trim the board to the required dimensions, you may need to pass it through the thicknesser several times. Most home-workshop machines are not equipped to plane or thickness boards wider than 150 mm; never attempt to remove the cutter guard in order to plane wider boards, because such a procedure is very dangerous.

The disposable cutting blades on the machine need replacing when the ridges are visible on the planed wood or when the shavings are uneven and burnished-looking. Keep the blades clean by rubbing them periodically with a cloth dampened in turpentine, lacquer thinner or a mixture of paraffin and oil.

A Dual-Function Machine for Perfect Edges

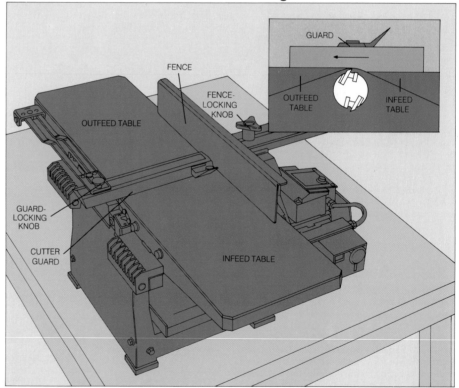

Anatomy of the planer. The planer, mounted here on a stationary base, has a work surface of 1000 by 260 mm. Its cutter head divides the infeed table nearer the operator, on the right, from the outfeed table, on the left; the fence spans both. The cutter guard is adjusted vertically or laterally, depending on which part of a board is being planed. For face planing, the guard should be fixed just above the board and extended all the way to the fence; for edge planing, it should be fixed just to the side of the board and lowered all the way to the outfeed table. The fence-locking knob can be loosened to tilt the fence at angles from 90 degrees to 45 degrees to serve as a guide in making chamfer and bevel cuts; the fence can also be moved laterally across the planing tables. The height-adjusting knob, which is positioned below the infeed table, is used for raising and lowering the infeed table and thus determining the depth of the cut (inset).

Anatomy of the thicknesser. With the planing tables swung back and a clip-on guard placed over the cutter head, the thicknesser is ready for use. The thicknessing table is raised or lowered to give the required cutting depth and to allow the board to travel through the feed mechanism. This consists of the cutter head itself and two spring-loaded rollers—one for drawing the timber into the blades, and one for drawing it out again *(inset)*. The infeed roller, which is driven by the same motor that powers the cutter head, can be adjusted for either fast or slow cutting.

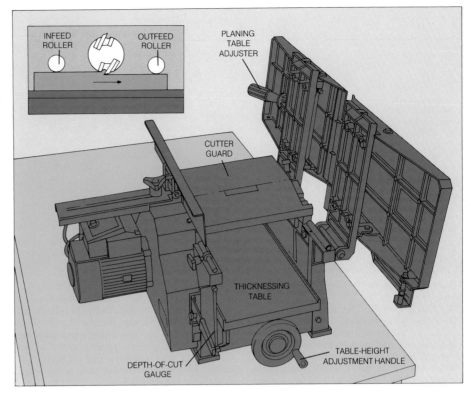

INFEED ROLLER
OUTFEED ROLLER
PLANING TABLE ADJUSTER
CUTTER GUARD
THICKNESSING TABLE
DEPTH-OF-CUT GAUGE
TABLE-HEIGHT ADJUSTMENT HANDLE

Planing the Face of a Board

1 Starting the cut. Adjust the height of the infeed table to give the required depth of cut. Place the board on the infeed table and secure the guard just above its upper face. Stand to the left of the infeed table, with your right hand at the back end of the board. Switch on the motor and feed the board forwards at a steady rate, pressing down and towards the fence with your left hand.

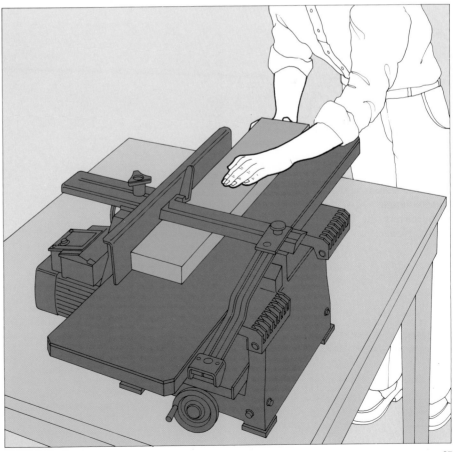

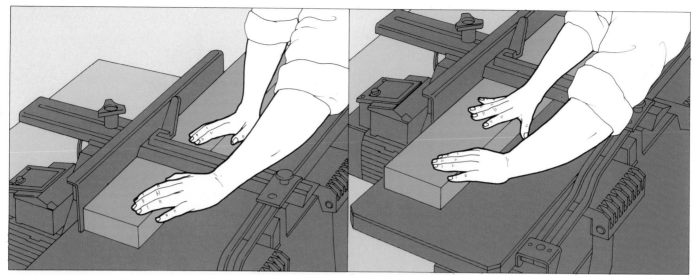

2 **Completing the cut.** As the board moves over the cutter, move round the side of the machine and place your left hand on the portion of the board now on the outfeed table. Maintain downward pressure—if you allow the board to lift at the front, you will not get an even surface. When about half the board has passed over the cutter, use both hands to push down and forwards on the portion over the outfeed table *(above, right)*, maintaining the pressure until the cut is finished. If a board is cupped, place it concave side down on the infeed table, and guide it over the cutter head as you would for normal planing. If a board is twisted, position it so that as large an area of the board as possible is in contact with the infeed table. Then plane as you would for a straight timber, pressing down on the parts of the board that are touching the table.

Planing the First Edge and the Ends

1 **Cutting a square edge.** Position the planed face of the board against the fence and adjust the guard so that it rests on the outfeed table and almost touches the opposite face. Place your right hand at the back end of the board and your left hand at a comfortable distance in front. Push the board forwards and down, moving it at a steady rate from the infeed to the outfeed table; keep both hands well away from the cutter head. Do not relax your pressure or change the slow, steady rate of feed until the cut is finished.

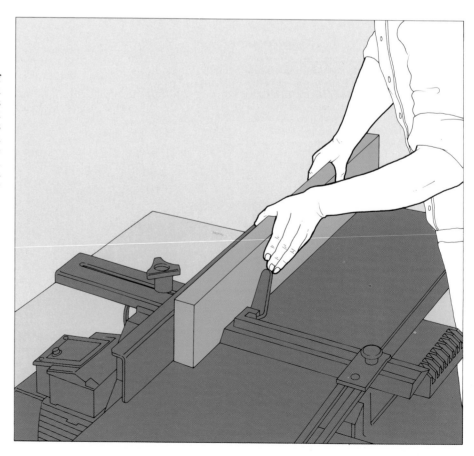

2 **Trimming the ends.** Place the board on end against the fence, with the guard adjusted as for planing an edge *(opposite page, Step 1)*. Steady the upright board with your left hand and push it forwards and down with your right. After cutting about 35 mm into the board *(inset)*, stop the forward motion and pull the board slowly back on to the infeed table. Reverse the board so that the uncut portion is facing away from you and feed it over the cutter head. This dual trimming eliminates splintering at the end of the cut. Trim the other end of the board in the same way.

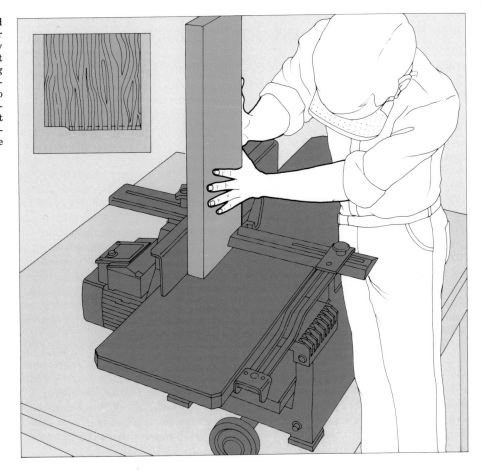

Using the Thicknesser

The correct sequence. Place the board, planed edge down, on the thicknessing table *(right)*. Raise or lower the table to give the required board width, and set the rollers to operate at the required speed. Switch on the machine and steady the board with your hands as it is fed under the cutter head. When the board has been trimmed to the correct width, place the planed face of the board on the table and repeat the procedure to give the required board thickness.

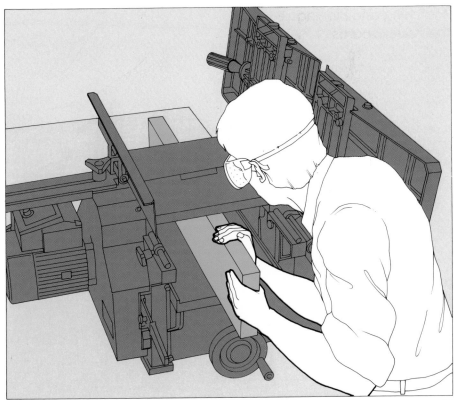

Jointing by Hand to Produce Wide Panels

Before plywood came into common use in the 1930s, large wood panels were made by fastening narrow boards together edge to edge. The simplest and most commonly used technique for such edge jointing, still used in fine cabinetwork, is to plane the edges of adjoining boards until they match exactly, and then glue them together. If the boards are of equal thickness, the resulting panel will be smooth on both sides, with nearly invisible joints that are as strong as the wood itself.

By carefully selecting and matching the boards to be jointed, you can make an apparently solid piece with a uniform grain pattern or a panel with alternating bands of wood colour and grain. Or you can use boards cut from a single thick block of wood (page 21, Step 2) to make a matched pattern in which adjacent boards seem to reflect each other.

When selecting the boards, choose well-seasoned wood to avoid shrinking, which could cause warping or opened joints. You can minimize the danger of warping in the finished panel by using narrow boards, 100 to 150 mm wide, and arranging them so that growth rings visible at the ends of adjoining boards curve in opposite directions. This ensures that the natural tendency of each board to cup towards its sapside (page 13) is counteracted by its neighbours, which are facing in the opposite direction.

The key to making perfect joints is careful edge planing. The technique of freehand planing with a jointer plane, 550 to 600 mm long, is similar to that used for planing the edge of any board, but the extra-long sole of the jointer plane helps to ensure a straight edge without bumps or dips. Freehand planing requires practice to yield perfect results; but it allows you to change the planing direction, if necessary, to deal with reversal of grain direction, and to make small variations in the depth of cut to match adjoining pieces.

Until you master freehand planing, you may want to use a shooting board (opposite). It guarantees a planed edge perpendicular to the surface of the board, and provides an automatic depth stop so you do not remove too much wood. It also allows you to use a plane with a sole shorter than that of the jointer plane.

Whichever planing method you use, be sure that the adjoining edges fit precisely. Any gap wide enough to allow light to pass through will greatly reduce the holding power of the glue.

White liquid glue, also known as polyvinyl acetate or PVA glue, is commonly used for edge jointing. It is strong, fills small gaps, and dries slowly enough to allow time for making fine adjustments. If greater moisture resistance is important, use a waterproof synthetic resin glue (urea-formaldehyde) instead.

Bar cramps, each with a pair of adjustable jaws mounted on a metal bar, are the best choice for clamping edge-jointed panels. It is advisable to clamp the panel up "dry" before applying glue to the board edges to ensure that all the edges fit nicely together. Place thin wood scraps between the edges of the panel and the jaws of the cramps to avoid bruising the wood. And in order to prevent stains that can be caused by a chemical reaction between the wood and the steel, put a sheet of paper between the metal bars and the wood wherever they might come into contact.

Matching and Planing the Panel Boards

1 **Laying out the panel.** Position selected boards on a flat surface and align them to achieve the best possible grain pattern. Use a pencil and a straightedge to draw three lines in a "crow's foot" shape from one side of the panel to the other, as a guide for maintaining the chosen grain pattern. Mark the ends of the boards at a point about 70 mm beyond the planned length of the finished panel, and cut off protruding boards at these marks to make them easier to handle.

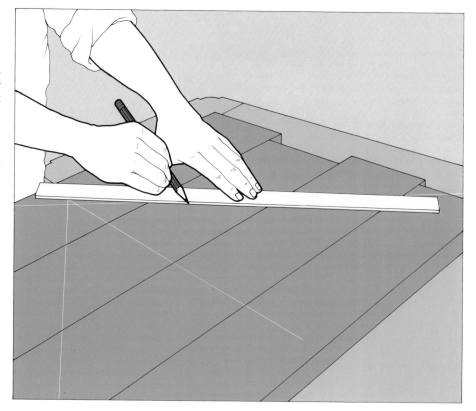

2 **Freehand edge planing.** Clamp a board from one side of the panel in a vice so that its inside edge faces upwards. Using a jointer plane or a jack plane, test the edge for the best planing direction *(page 10)*, then begin at one end and plane the entire length. Gripping the nose of the plane with one hand will help ensure that the edge and the face of the board form a 90-degree angle. When the edge is straight and square, plane the matching edge of the next board in the same manner.

3 **Testing matched edges.** With one board clamped in the vice, planed edge up, set the planed edge of the matching board on top of it with the crow's-foot marks aligned. Check the joint for nicks, gouges, and any gaps where light is visible. Use a pencil to mark the areas that need more work, then plane wood away until the edges match perfectly. Use the same techniques to plane and match the remaining pairs of edges in the panel.

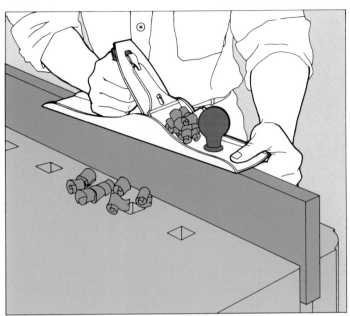

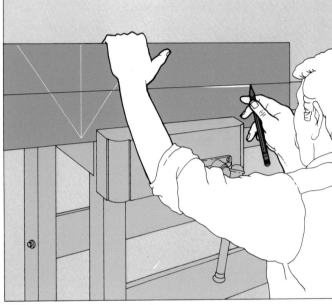

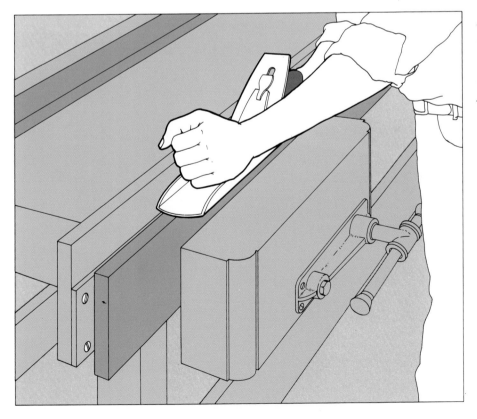

A Simple Jig for Cutting a Straight Edge

Planing with a shooting board. Position the panel board to be edge-planed next to a shooting-board jig; clamp both in a vice, with the edge to be planed slightly higher than the depth stop of the shooting board. Plane from one end of the panel board to the other, keeping the side of the plane flush against the shooting board. Put wax or linseed oil on the side and bottom of the plane if there is a need to reduce friction.

To make a shooting board, cut a depth stop of 3 mm tempered hardboard, 80 mm wide and as long as the panel board, with one perfectly straight edge. Glue and screw this depth stop to the face of a straight 25 by 150 mm board as long as the panel board, positioning the straight edge of the depth stop on top and keeping the bottom edges of the two pieces aligned.

Gluing for Smooth Beauty

1 **Assembling the panel.** Stand two bar cramps on a perfectly flat and level surface and cover the bars with paper. Position the boards on the cramps, noting the alignment of the crow's-foot marks and attempting to match the grain patterns on adjacent boards. Tighten the two cramps enough to hold the boards in position, but without exerting pressure on them.

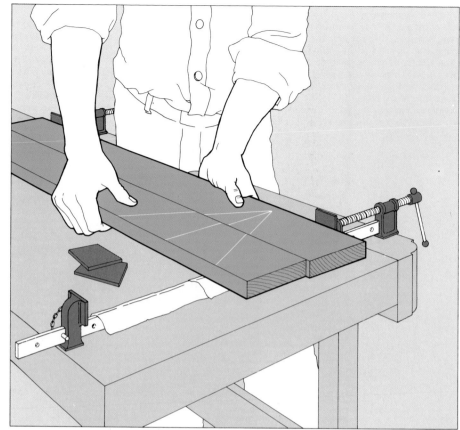

2 **Checking the fit.** Place a third bar cramp upside down on top of the boards in the centre of the panel. Tighten all three cramps little by little until light pressure is exerted. Check the fit of all the joints. Dismantle the panel; if necessary, re-plane any badly fitting edges. Then apply a thin coat of glue to the board edges and reassemble the panel as before.

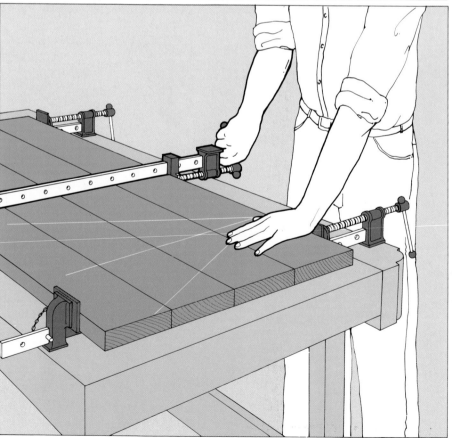

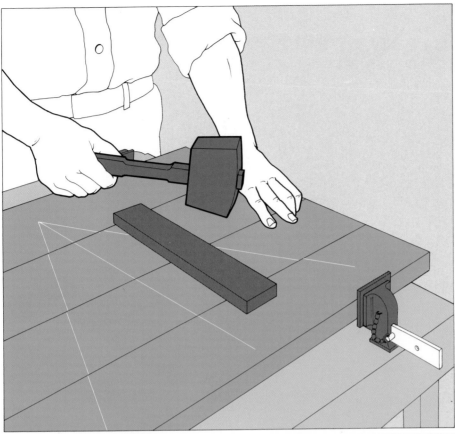

3 **Adjusting the glued boards.** Tighten the bar cramps lightly against the glued panel. If any board is too high, lay a scrap length of wood across the boards and tap gently with a wooden mallet until the raised board is flush with its neighbours. Continue to adjust until the entire panel surface is flush. Tighten the bar cramps until a thin bead of glue is squeezed out of each joint. Clean this excess glue from the panel with a damp rag.

Store the glued and clamped panel flat to keep it from twisting as the glue dries. You can also store it by leaning it against a wall, but make sure all the cramp ends are resting against the wall and the floor. Allow the glue to set completely. Release the bar cramps, beginning with the centre one.

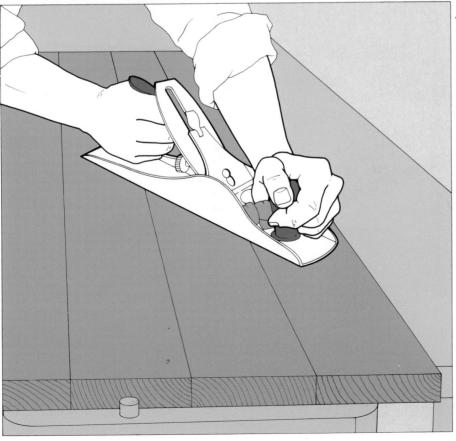

4 **Final smoothing.** Use a straightedge to check the flatness of the assembled panel *(page 23)*. Plane down any high spots diagonally across the grain. Give a final smoothing with the plane set for very fine shavings, planing parallel to the long grain.

If the panel is to be planed to a desired thickness, mark lines accordingly around the edges and proceed as on page 25, Step 2.

A Choice of Connections

The quality of a piece of furniture is judged by the beauty of its form and the strength of its parts—and joinery plays a major role in both. More than just a means of locking together two pieces of wood, a joint can merge component parts with grace or set them off in fine contrast to each other. It can guide the eye along the lines of a piece, as in a mitre joint, which allows the grain to flow unbroken round the corner; or it can delineate the change of direction, as in a lap joint. It can combine in itself both function and aesthetics, arresting the eye with such intricate details as the wing-like wedges of the dovetail joint or the contrasting wood of exposed dowel joints. Conversely, a joint may exert no visual effect at all, being completely hidden—as the invisible mortise and tenon joint is.

Faced with a multitude of choices, most woodworkers elect to use the simplest, strongest joint appropriate to the job. All joints, regardless of how they are cut, derive some of their strength from the amount of gluing surface they provide. The strongest joints are those that connect two pieces of wood in a way that bonds the greatest possible surface of lengthwise grain on each piece. The long grain, running with the wood fibres, holds glue in suspension, ensuring a strong bond; the end grain, cutting across the fibres, is so porous that it simply absorbs the glue and offers practically no gripping surface. Some joints do not expose as much long grain as others. A mitre joint, for example, cuts diagonally across the end grain and usually has to be reinforced with a spline to increase its holding power.

In fact, because most joints can be given the requisite strength, the choice of joint usually boils down to how much time and skill it takes to cut and fit it. Hand-cut dovetails take considerably longer to make than machine-cut dovetails, and machine-cut mortise and tenon joints are simpler and speedier still—which is why most craftsmen choose them. But even the simple joints demand precision cutting. No woodworker should cheat on the time spent in marking and measuring the cut. Sharp hand tools and well-honed power-tool blades and bits are also essential to the clean cuts of good joinery.

Finally, for a joint to be both smooth and serviceable, its parts must fit together as precisely as possible. In a good joint, no light shows between the pieces—proof that the gluing surfaces mate. The snugness of fit should be such that some hand pressure is needed to bring the pieces together, or a light tap with a mallet or a hammer and block. But the fit should not be so tight as to cause the wood to split. In earlier days, the strength of a joint depended primarily upon the tight fit of its interlocking parts. Today, wood screws and sophisticated glues can supplement fit, not only strengthening the joint but increasing its life expectancy.

The Tongue and Groove Joint and Its Variations

Cutting a groove in one board and fitting a projecting tongue from another into it is one of the oldest and still one of the best ways to make a strong wood joint. Two types of cut are used to make such a joint. One is the rectangular channel, called a groove, cut in either the edge or the face of a board. The other is a step-like cut, called a rebate, made in the edge of a board. In a variation of the basic rebate, two shallow rebate cuts may be made, one along each side of a board edge, leaving a projecting centre remnant, called the tongue. Grooves and rebates can be combined in several ways to join boards, either at right angles or flush with each other (below).

The tools which are most commonly used for making these cuts are the router and the spindle moulder. Each has advantages in certain circumstances. For example, if you are cutting grooves and rebates in wide boards, plywood sheets, oddly shaped pieces or warped wood, the router is a better choice, since the wood remains stationary while the tool follows its contours. In these circumstances a spindle moulder may fail to cut consistently deep, especially if the wood is warped. Moreover, it takes time to adjust the spindle moulder to the correct cutting height and depth, and there are more opportunities for careless mistakes to be made. Nevertheless, once a cutter is installed and adjusted, the spindle moulder will be faster than a router if you wish to produce identical cuts in a number of boards.

No matter which tool you choose, precise measurements are imperative. A keen eye and a perfectly straight rule are needed to make certain the cutting blades are precisely positioned. But even after careful measuring, every new blade setting should be tested on scrap wood. This extra effort pays dividends, especially if you are making intricate cuts like those in a lock joint (page 42). To prevent plywood from splintering when cut with a spindle moulder, you can either score the wood before you begin with a blade set very low, or cover the location of the cut with a strip of masking tape.

If your project calls for a large amount of edge-to-edge joinery, the double tongue and groove joint is a convenient alternative to the single version. To make it with a spindle moulder, you will need to install two identical blades separated by a distance equivalent to the blade thickness. In a single pass, these shape pairs of tongues and grooves in the edge of a board. Furthermore, without changing the adjustment you can shape the edge of the board that will be joined to the first one.

Six Rebate and Groove Cuts

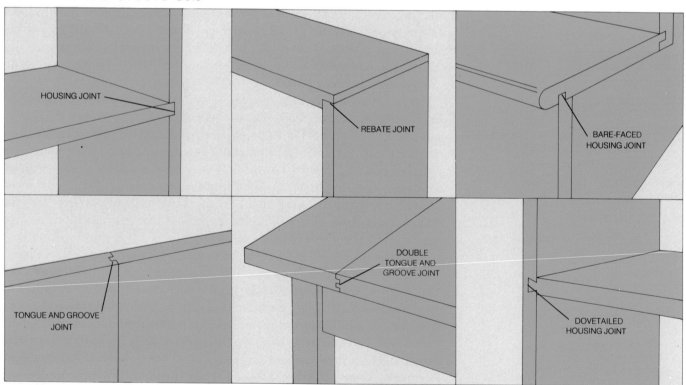

A catalogue of joints. The basic housing joint, shown in the drawing as it is used to hold shelves, is formed when the square end of one board is fitted into a channel-like housing in a second board. A simple rebate joint, here used at the top corner of a box, is made by fitting the unshaped end of one board into the rebated end of the other. A rebate and a groove may also be combined to form a bare-faced housing joint with the rebated end of one board fitting into the groove of another, shown here as it is used in a stair tread.

The tongue and groove joint, common in flooring and panelling, joins edges; a groove in the edge of one board holds the tongue left by cutting two shallow rebates in the other. The double tongue and groove joint is made with two blades spaced apart; pairs of tongues and grooves provide interlocking gluing surfaces. A sixth joint, the dove-tailed housing, combines the strength of a conventional tongue and groove joint with the structural rigidity of a dovetail.

Routing Out Grooves and Recessed Edges

Routing a groove. A made-to-measure jig makes a useful guide when you rout a groove across the face of a board. First mark the position and depth of the groove, then hook the jig over the board. To position the jig, raise the cutting bit above the router base, place the router in the jig, then move jig and router together until the bit lines up with the groove position. Clamp the jig and the wood in place. Switch on the router, lower the bit into the near crosspiece to the desired depth and move it into the board. Lift it out when a notch has been cut into the jig's far crosspiece.

Make the jig of smooth-edged wood about 75 mm wide and as thick as the board being cut. Use a square to position the jig pieces at right angles, then fasten them with screws. The two long braces of the jig should be spaced apart exactly the width of the router base.

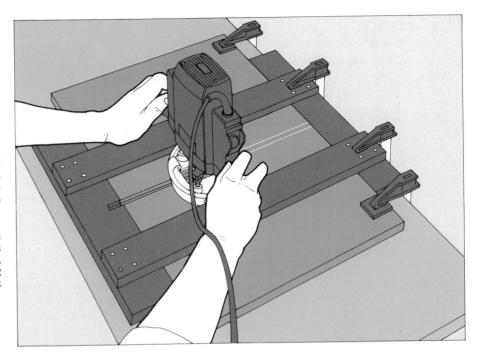

Safety Rules for Routers

The high speed of the router's rotating bit demands that this portable tool be treated with the same respect as larger, stationary power tools. In addition to the general safety rules for all power tools *(page 14)*, observe these specific precautions for the router:

☐ Switch off and unplug the tool before installing or removing a bit, and make sure that the cutter is secure after it has been installed.

☐ Anchor your work with cramps or nails, so that both hands are left free to guide the tool.

☐ Run the power cable over one shoulder to keep it well clear of the bit.

☐ Let the bit reach full speed before beginning a cut, and raise the bit from the work before switching the router off. But keep in mind that the cutter will continue to spin for several seconds after the router is switched off.

☐ Whenever possible, move the router away from you and direct it so that the leading edge of the bit, which spins clockwise, is biting into new wood; position any guides or jigs in such a way that they will counteract the resulting anticlockwise torque.

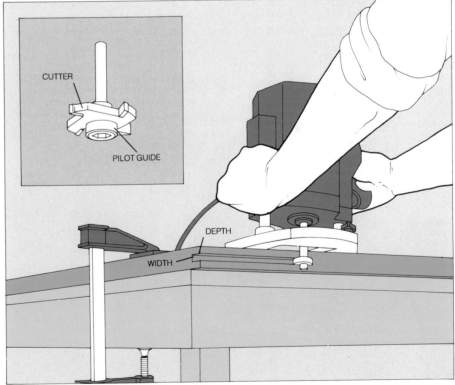

A bit for routing edge grooves. A special groove cutter, called a panel-grooving bit or a spline bit, is fitted with a non-cutting pilot guide at its tip. This guide rolls along a board edge to ensure that the groove will be of uniform depth. To use this bit, mark the position of the groove, clamp the wood to a worktable edge, and lower the cutter until it lines up with the marks. Guide the bit into the wood from left to right. If you are cutting wood of a kind that may chip or splinter, such as plywood, begin the cut about 25 mm from the left end, and finish the remnant by cutting from right to left.

The groove's width will be determined by the size of the cutter which is used; its depth depends on the diameter of the pilot *(inset)*. Choose a small pilot for making a deep cut and a large one for making a shallow cut.

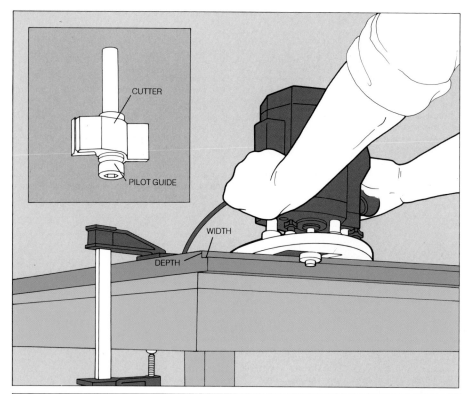

Routing rebates and tongues. A rebate cutter equipped with a pilot guide *(inset)* is used in the same way as the panel-grooving bit *(page 37, below)*. Select a cutter-pilot combination that will produce a rebate of the desired depth and width. Cut from left to right, but in this operation lower the bit gradually so that each pass removes no more than 8 mm of wood.

For a tongue of wood on the edge of a board or panel, mark and cut two rebates, one in each opposing face, so that the projection remaining is centred and has the desired thickness. Use a cutter-pilot combination that cuts a rebate 2 mm narrower than the depth of the groove.

Routing a Dovetailed Tongue and Groove

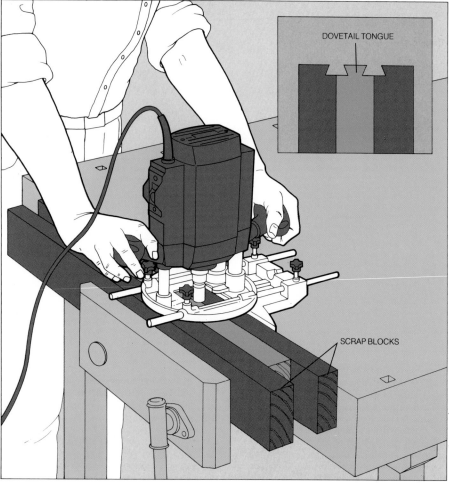

Support blocks for the bit. Fit the router with a dovetail cutter bit of the desired size and cut the groove using a jig as shown on page 37. Do not lower the splayed cutter directly into the board or lift it away while the groove is being cut—feed the router, with the cutter lowered, into the outside edge of the jig and, in a single pass, cut the groove through the board and the far crosspiece.

Clamp the board in which the tongue is to be cut in the vice with two blocks of scrap wood, one on either side, flush with its end. The scrap blocks must be identical in width, and their edges should project about 50 mm beyond the workpiece to provide support for the router fence at either end. Mark the outline of the tongue on the edge of the board. Fit the side fence to the router and adjust it so that, when the fence is butted against the outer face of one of the scrap blocks, the bit will cut a groove through the workpiece and the scrap block, its inner edge thus forming one side of the tongue *(inset)*.

To cut the opposite side of the tongue, run the router fence along the outer face of the second scrap block. As when cutting the groove, the cutter must be in the lowered position before being fed into the edge of the board; at the end of the cut, do not lift the cutter until it is completely clear of the workpiece.

The Spindle Moulder: Precise Cutting Along a Board Edge

Anatomy of a spindle moulder. Used for moulding edges, shaping curves and dovetailing as well as for fashioning tongues and grooves, the spindle moulder is a versatile addition to the home workshop. The appropriate cutter for the job is slotted on to a vertical spindle that projects from the machined metal worktable; when the machine is switched on, the spindle and cutter revolve at high speeds to cut the edge of the workpiece which is fed along the table.

Adjustable guards hold the workpiece against the worktable and fence and protect you from the cutter. When cutting grooves and rebates in a straight edge, the infeed and outfeed fences are exactly aligned and an auxiliary fence *(page 40, Step 2)* ensures that the cutting blade is exposed no more than is necessary for the cut you are making. When the entire edge of a board is being trimmed, the outfeed fence is moved forwards and repositioned to guide the cut edge in the same way as the outfeed table of a power planer *(page 26)*. Many worktables also incorporate a channel for a mitre gauge.

Cutters useful for edge-to-edge jointing include the adjustable grooving blade, which works on the same principle as a table saw "wobble" blade described on pages 54–55; the carbide-tipped solid grooving blade, which is available in a range of thicknesses to cut grooves of different widths; and a cutter block fitted with straight blades for cutting rebates. The cutter block can be fitted with a wide range of different shaped blades to cut complex mouldings.

Spacers and rings set into the worktable are slotted on to the spindle above and below the cutter, and the assembly is secured by tightening a locknut. The height of the chosen cutter in relation to the workpiece can be adjusted as required by turning a handle.

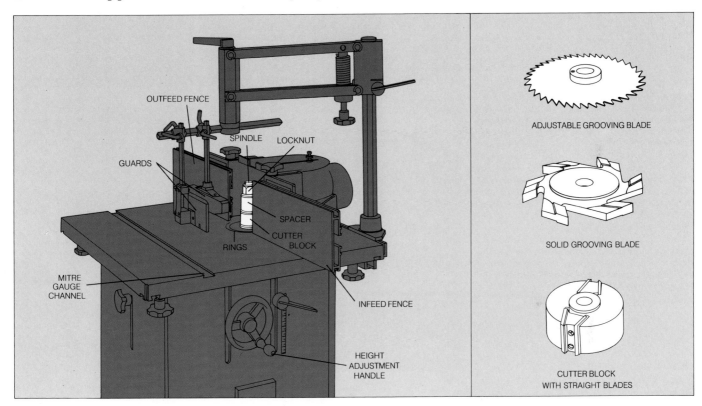

OUTFEED FENCE

SPINDLE LOCKNUT

GUARDS

SPACER

CUTTER BLOCK

RINGS

MITRE GAUGE CHANNEL

INFEED FENCE

HEIGHT ADJUSTMENT HANDLE

ADJUSTABLE GROOVING BLADE

SOLID GROOVING BLADE

CUTTER BLOCK WITH STRAIGHT BLADES

Safety Rules for the Spindle Moulder

Alertness and a strict regard for safety precautions are required when operating the spindle moulder. Proper guarding of the cutter blade is of paramount importance. In addition to the general safety rules for all power tools *(page 14)*, observe the following precautions:

☐ To protect hands from the cutters, wherever possible use the guards fitted to the machine. Install a faceboard if the machine has no auxiliary fence.

☐ For any operation where the machine's guard cannot be used, exercise extreme care. Use improvised guards and springboards, and feed the work with push sticks or blocks.

☐ Tighten the spindle locknut securely after fitting cutters. Regularly check the tightness of bolts holding cutter blades in blocks, and periodically check the threads and seatings: replace any that are worn or stretched.

☐ When using a collar to follow a template, ensure that the workpiece is securely fitted to the template.

☐ Do not exceed the speed recommended by the blade manufacturer for the cutter you are using.

☐ Whenever possible, set up the machine so that you will be cutting the underside of the workpiece.

☐ Use a jig or push stick to feed small workpieces past the cutter blades.

Tonguing and Grooving on the Spindle Moulder

1 Setting the blade height. Fit a solid grooving blade to cut a groove of the desired width on to the spindle. Add spacers and the locknut, and tighten the nut firmly. Select a piece of scrap timber the same thickness as the boards to be joined and on one edge draw two lines to mark the position of the groove. Lay this board on the machine table and offer it up to the stationary saw blade. Adjust the height of the blade by turning the spindle height adjustment wheel until the tips of the blade are aligned with the lines marked on the board edge *(right)*.

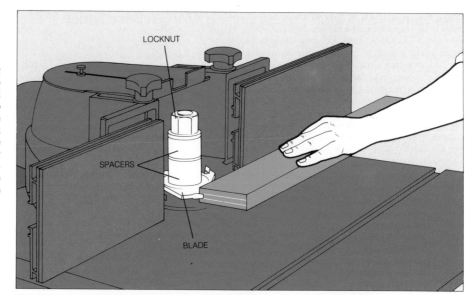

2 Setting the groove depth. Loosen the fence locking nuts and pull both halves of the fence forwards until they are in front of the spindle and clear of the blade. To make a faceboard or auxiliary fence, align the two halves of the fence and secure a 12 mm plywood board across them. Switch the machine on and, with the blade spinning, place one hand on each end of the fence and slowly push the fence back towards the blade. When the blade cuts a slot in the faceboard and the tips protrude about 10 mm, switch off the machine and apply the blade brake.

Adjust the fence until the tips of the saw blade protrude through the slot in the faceboard by the desired depth of the groove, measuring with a rule butted against the faceboard *(right)*. Fix the fence firmly by tightening the locking nuts.

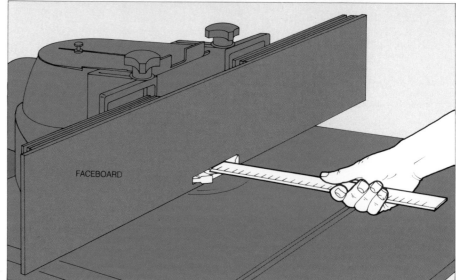

3 Cutting the groove. With the machine switched off, lay the marked length of scrap board against the faceboard on the infeed side of the table. Install the guard, adjusting its top and side blocks so that the board is gently held against the table and faceboard but can be passed through easily. Switch the machine on and feed the scrap board through the guard to cut the groove. Do not stand in a direct line with the workpiece. Use your right hand to push the end of the board, holding it against the faceboard with your left *(right)*; as you approach the end of the cut, transfer first your left and then your right hand to the outfeed side of the table to guide the board through.

Measure the cut board to check that the groove is central, and adjust the height of the blade if necessary. Cut the groove in the board to be joined in the same way as the scrap timber. If you are joining a number of boards, cut all the grooves required before resetting the machine to cut the tongues.

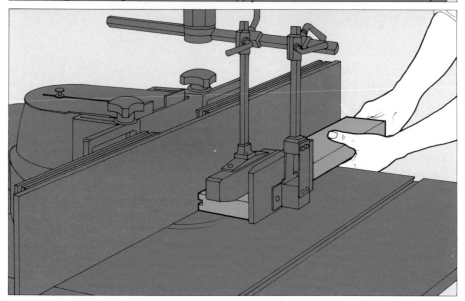

4 **Fitting the cutter block.** Switch off the machine, release the fence locking nuts and pull the fence forwards clear of the blade. Unscrew the spindle locknut and remove it, together with the spacers and the grooving blade. Fit a cutter block with straight blades on to the spindle, add a spacer if necessary, and replace and tighten the locknut. Lower the spindle until the tops of the cutter blades are slightly lower than the grooving blade was. Switch on the machine and push back the faceboard so that the cutter blades remove the wood below the slot in the faceboard; then switch the machine off.

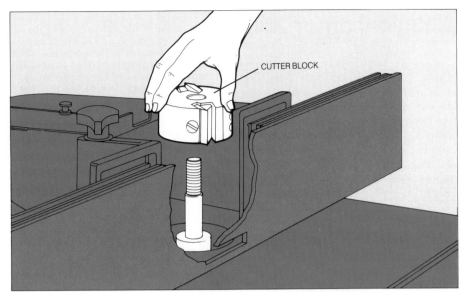

5 **Adjusting the cutter block.** To set the depth of cut, move the fence until the cutter blades project through the faceboard about a millimetre less than the depth of the groove you have already cut. Lock the fence in position. To set the width of the rebate which is to be cut, lay a grooved board against the faceboard and adjust the spindle height until the top of the cutter blades is aligned with the lower edge of the groove.

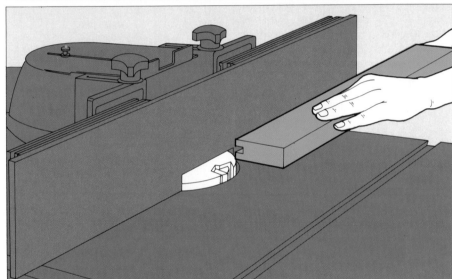

6 **Testing the fit.** Adjust the guard, switch on the machine, and feed a scrap board the same thickness as the boards being joined past the cutter to cut a rebate. Turn the board over and feed it past the cutter a second time to cut the second rebate, thus forming the tongue. Switch off the machine and test the fit of the tongue in the groove already cut *(inset)*—the tongue should fit snugly in the groove, yet slide in easily. If the joint is too tight, raise the cutter block slightly to make the tongue narrower; if it is too loose, lower the cutter block. After adjustment, cut another tongue in scrap wood and recheck the fit. When a good fit is achieved, cut all the tongues required in the boards to be joined.

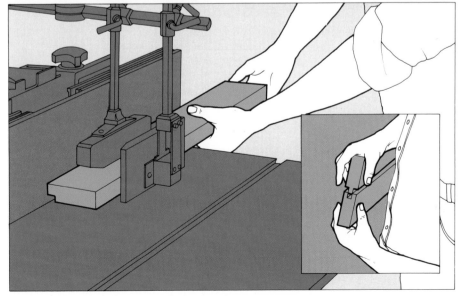

A Rigid Corner Joint

A strategic combination of tongue and groove cuts gives strength to a corner joint by increasing its glue area while locking the joint in every direction but one. The half-blind lock joint shown here is sometimes used for attaching drawer fronts, since the joint is hidden from view and resists being pulled apart as the drawer is opened. Although not suitable for corners visible from two sides, this joint may be used where a dovetail's strength *(page 44)* is not needed.

The most convenient power tool for cutting housings and trimming tongues is a spindle moulder. The machine is used in the same way as for making joints in the edges of boards to form a flat surface *(pages 40–41)*; however, because the machine's guard cannot be used when a board is held upright on the worktable, you will have to use an improvised guard known as a springboard *(opposite page)*.

Make sure the boards to be joined are straight, smooth and squarely cut. Mark each face and edge so that you can keep track of the final positions.

The joint is started with a wide housing that becomes the reference point for all subsequent cuts. Mark the position of each cut as the work progresses and adjust the blade carefully, always testing with scrap pieces the same thickness as the work. Check a finished housing with a rule and with the piece that will fit into it.

1 Mapping the joint. On a piece of paper or scrap wood, make a full-scale drawing of the joint; number the cuts *(inset)*. This preliminary task will make it easier for you to visualize how the joint you are making is going to work in the finished product.

Mark the width and the depth of the two housings. The width of the tongue that covers the front of the joint should match the width of the tongue that fits in the inside housing. You can vary dimensions, however, to suit the thickness and kind of wood you are using; the dimensions which are given below are for two pieces of 25 mm timber.

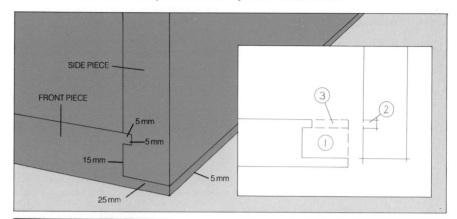

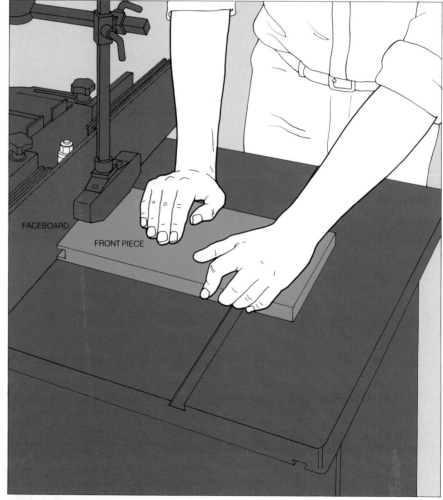

2 Cutting the wide housing. Fit a 15 mm grooving blade on to the spindle and adjust the blade height to 5 mm. Align the infeed and outfeed fences and secure a faceboard across them *(page 40, Step 2)*. Adjust the faceboard until the blade projects 25 mm, then tighten the fence bolts. Install the guard and run a piece of scrap wood through the machine to test the dimensions of the cut. Adjust the blade if necessary, then cut the front piece of the drawer.

3 **Cutting the second housing.** Stand the front piece of the drawer on edge and butt the side piece against it, aligning the inside surface of the front tongue with the end of the side piece. Mark the place at which the rear tongue meets the side piece *(below, left)*; this mark indicates where you will make the second housing cut.

Fit a 5 mm blade to the spindle and adjust it to the correct height and depth for the second housing. To make a springboard to hold the work against the fence while you push it past the cutters, mitre the end of a 400 mm long piece of 100 by 50 mm timber at a 45-degree angle, then cut saw kerfs 3 mm apart and roughly 125 mm deep in that end. Before you cut the housing, sandwich a scrap of wood—the same thickness as the work—between the springboard and the fence. Clamp the springboard to the table, and brace it with a 100 by 50 mm piece of timber—clamped at a right angle. The springboard and the brace should be adjusted so that the scrap will move smoothly in a forward direction but will not move backwards.

Test the accuracy of the cut you have made with the piece of scrap wood, adjusting the blade if necessary, and then cut the housing in the side of the drawer *(below, right)*.

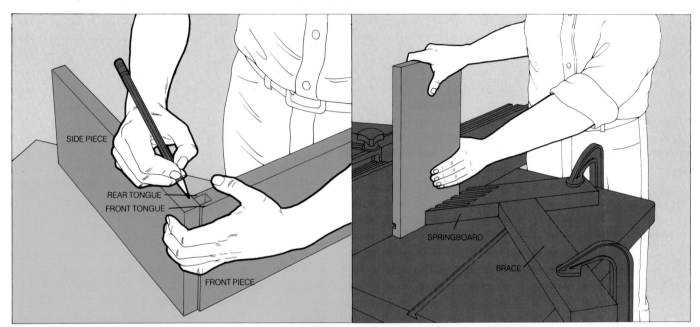

4 **Trimming the rear tongue.** Stand the front piece on edge and hold the edge of the side piece at a right angle to it, lining up the second housing with the rear tongue and aligning the inside face of the side piece with the bottom surface of the first housing. When all four surfaces are in alignment, insert a pencil in the second housing and make a pencil mark at the point where the housing's bottom surface meets the rear tongue *(above, left)*. This mark indicates the position of the trim line for the rear tongue.

Measure the distance along the rear tongue to the trim line. Adjust the height of the blade to this distance, and its depth to cut a few millimetres more than the thickness of the rear tongue. Adjust the springboard and make a test cut on a piece of scrap wood. Check for accuracy, then trim the rear tongue on the drawer front *(above, right)*.

When the cuts for the joints at both ends of the front piece have been completed, assemble the joint. First apply white PVA to all of the interlocking surfaces. Clamp the joints and wipe away the excess glue *(inset)*.

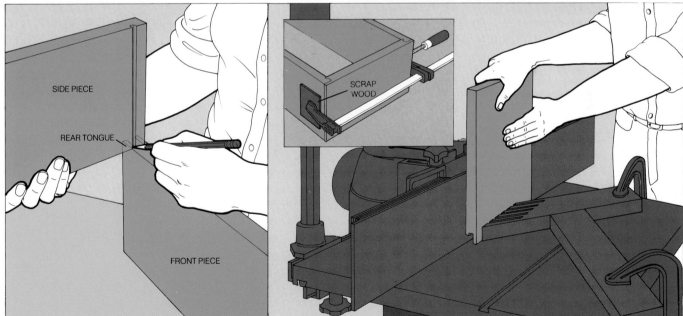

A Hand-Cut Joint with Interlocking Tails

The interlocking parts of a dovetail joint are a triumph of the woodworker's art. Often used for decorative effect at the corners of boxes or cabinets, dovetails can be equally useful when hidden away on the sides of drawers, since they are among the strongest of corner joints. Uniform dovetails may be made quickly with a special template and a router or power drill (*pages 50–53*). The more time-consuming handwork, however, permits you to make a wider variety of sizes and shapes as well as to demonstrate your skill.

A fine-toothed, straight-cutting saw and sharp wood chisels are the main tools used for cutting dovetails. A Gents saw or a dovetail saw equipped with tiny teeth that have very little set (deflection from the line of the blade) are best for making the kind of smooth, accurate cuts required. You should have several chisels of different widths: always cut with the widest chisel that will fit without breaking the corners of the delicate tails and sockets. Chisels with bevelled sides allow cutting into the corners of angled sockets.

Clean, well-fitting joints begin with accurate measuring and marking. The spur of your marking gauge should have a knifelike point so that it cuts a thin, straight mark; sharpen it with a file if necessary. Some woodworkers like to use a pencil gauge, made by drilling a hole to accept a pencil in the beam of a marking gauge at the opposite end to the spur. Use a sharp pencil to mark other lines, and further ensure accuracy by always cutting along the side of a line towards the waste wood you are removing. You can always shave wood away to make a tight joint fit better, but there is no good way of adding wood to a loose joint. If your saw wanders off a line when you are cutting a tail, finish the cut in a straight line. Absolute accuracy is not essential when cutting tails. When cutting the sockets to fit the tails, however, there is no margin for error.

Since most dovetail joints are part of a rectangular assembly you will cut and fit four joints before gluing and clamping any of them. Mark the matching pieces of each joint before you begin cutting, for easy identification at later stages. If your plan calls for a bottom or a back that will be set in a groove, cut the groove after cutting the joints, and add the bottom or back when you glue the unit together.

Two Versions of a Classic Connection

Through and lap dovetail joints. The simplest and strongest dovetail joint is the through dovetail *(right, above)*, which exposes end grain on both sides of the joint. Here the interlocking of the angled tails with the narrower pins on the socket piece *(inset)* gives the joint great holding power. The angle of the tails is generally 1:6 for softwoods and 1:8 for hardwoods. The pins are cut at least 6 mm wide on their narrow sides and are spaced no more than 80 mm apart, measuring from centre to centre.

In the lap dovetail *(right, below)*, the end grain of the tail piece is hidden by closed sockets. The tails, cut at least 6 mm shorter than the thickness of the socket piece, are otherwise identical with those in the through dovetail.

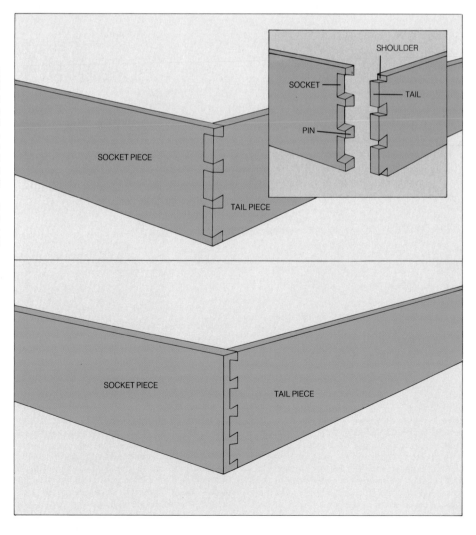

Cutting a Through Dovetail

1 Marking thickness for tails and pins. Set a marking gauge to match the thickness of the socket piece, and use it to scribe a line on all sides of the end of the tail piece. Then reset the marking gauge, this time to the thickness of the tail piece, and scribe a line on both sides of the matching end of the socket piece.

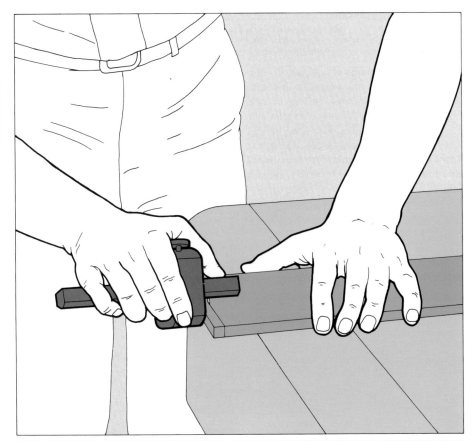

2 Laying out the tails. Lay out the positions of the tails with squared lines across the end of the tail piece; then use a sliding bevel, set to the desired angle, to extend the lines along the side of the tail piece to the marking-gauge line. In laying out the tails, first establish the outer corners by marking two lines across the end of the tail piece; position each line so that its distance from the corners is equal to half the thickness of the socket piece. Divide the space between these two lines into equal sections for the tails, leaving at least 6 mm for pins between adjacent tails.

If you are making several joints, you can speed the work of laying out the tails by using a homemade template. Make the template from hardwood (*left inset*) or aluminium cut to the required angle with shears (*right inset*).

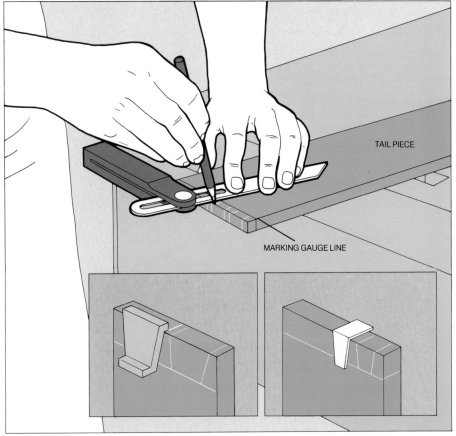

TAIL PIECE

MARKING GAUGE LINE

3 **Cutting the tails and shoulders.** Clamp the tail piece in a vice so that the lines on one side of each tail are exactly vertical *(right, above)*, and use a Gents or dovetail saw to cut carefully down the waste side of each vertical line as far as the marking-gauge line. Then change the position of the tail piece in the vice so that the remaining lines are vertical, and cut down each of these lines in the same way.

Reposition the tail piece in the vice so that the marking-gauge line is vertical *(right, below)*, and use the saw to cut along the marking-gauge line from the edge of the piece to the cut at the base of the first tail. Reclamp the piece with the opposite edge up, and cut the other shoulder.

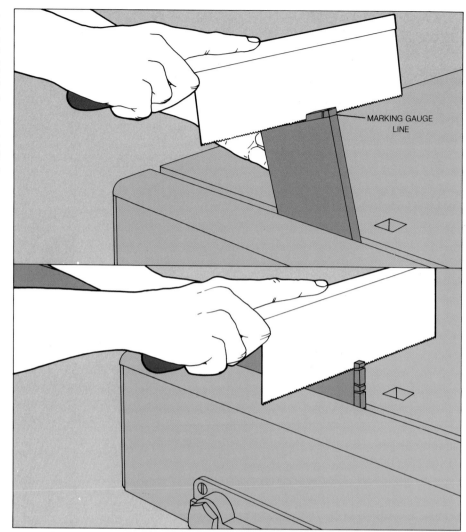

MARKING GAUGE LINE

4 **Cutting out the waste.** Clamp the tail piece vertically in the vice and use a coping saw to cut out as much of the waste wood between the tails as possible. Begin each cut in a saw kerf beside one tail, and cut to the kerf beside the adjacent tail, using extreme caution to avoid sawing below the marking-gauge line. If you find it difficult to control the saw, grip the handle with both hands.

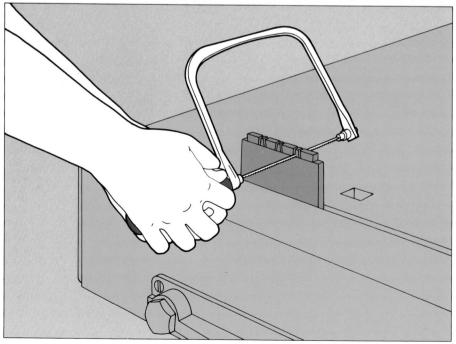

5 **Chiselling out the waste.** Clamp the tail piece on top of scrap wood on a flat work surface, and use a sharp bevel-edged chisel to cut away the remaining waste between the tails. Position the chisel edge on the marking-gauge line, bevel facing out, and tap it lightly with a mallet. Cut down to about half the width of the board, then chisel out waste between the other tails in the same way. Turn the tail piece over and reclamp it, then chisel out the waste from that side until all the spaces between the tails are clear.

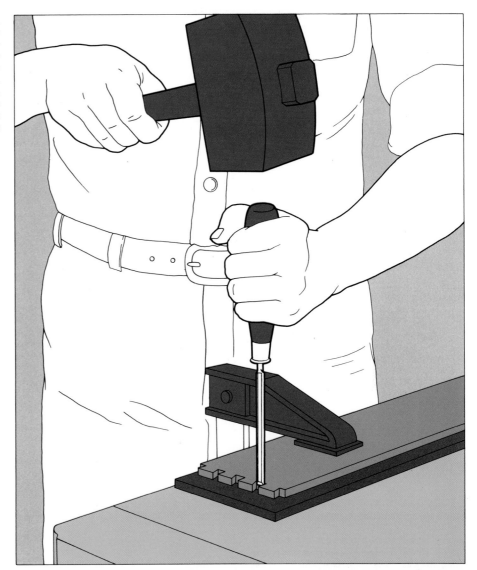

6 **Marking the socket piece.** Clamp the socket piece in a vice so that the amount exposed above the work surface is equal to the thickness of a support block of scrap wood. Position the tail piece on the scrap block so that the tails are aligned with the end of the socket piece. Holding the tail piece firmly against the socket piece, use a sharp pencil, a bradawl or a marking knife to trace the outline of the tails on the end of the socket piece. Then remove the tail piece and use a try square to continue the lines down each side of the socket piece to the marking-gauge line.

Use a dovetail saw to cut along the waste side of the marked lines down to the marking-gauge line, then use a coping saw to cut away as much of the waste as possible. Use a chisel and a mallet to cut out the remaining waste from each socket.

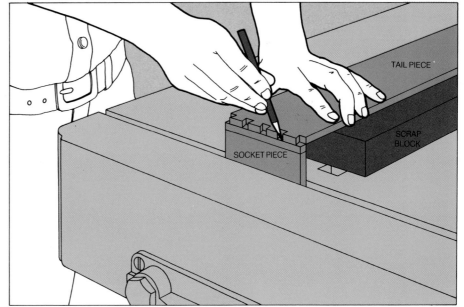

TAIL PIECE

SCRAP BLOCK

SOCKET PIECE

7 Fitting the joint. Clamp the socket piece vertically in the vice, position the tails in the sockets, and tap the tail piece lightly with a mallet to test the fit of the joint; use a piece of scrap wood on top of the tail piece to distribute the pressure evenly. There should be some friction in the joint, but if it is too tight to be seated with light tapping, dismantle it and use a chisel to slice thin shavings from the sides of the sockets.

After cutting and fitting all the joints in a unit, cover the contacting surfaces of each joint with a thin coat of PVA glue. Then put the unit together and use bar cramps to apply light pressure across the tail piece *(inset)*.

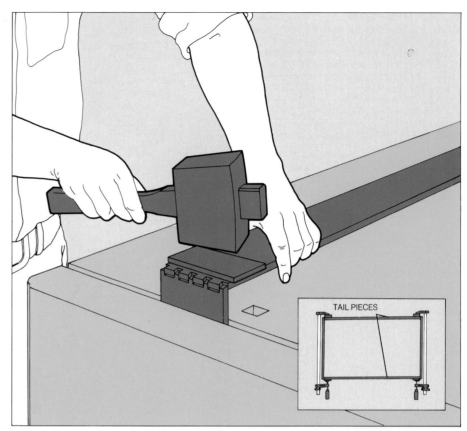

TAIL PIECES

Cutting a Lap Dovetail

1 Cutting the sockets. After cutting a tail piece with tails shorter than the thickness of the socket piece *(pages 45–47, Steps 1 to 5)*, clamp the socket piece vertically in the vice with a scrap board behind it; this prevents vibration when chiselling. Mark the outline of the tails on the end of the socket piece *(page 47, Step 6)*, then use a try square to continue the lines down the inside of the socket piece to the marking-gauge line. With a dovetail saw, cut the sides of each socket, holding the saw at an angle so that it follows the angled line on the end of the socket piece as well as the straight line on the side *(inset)*.

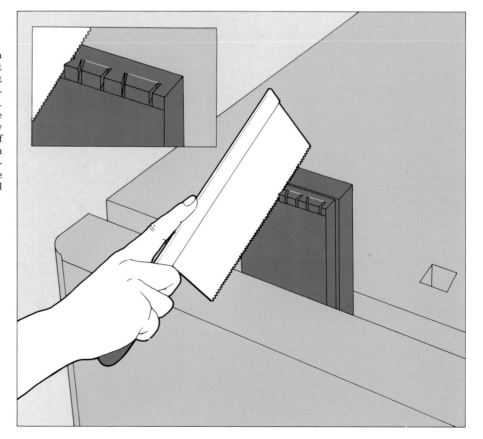

2 **Chiselling out the sockets.** Hold a sharp bevel-edged chisel horizontally, close to the top of the socket *(below)*; tap lightly with the mallet to cut straight across the grain. Work down as far as the marking-gauge line by making further small cuts, about 2 or 3 mm at a time. Then, with the chisel vertical *(bottom)*, cut down the grain on the pencil line to remove the waste wood. Do not attempt to chisel into the corners of the sockets, as this risks breaking the edges of the pins.

3 **Clearing out the corners.** Use a narrow chisel with bevelled sides to remove the waste in the corners of each socket. Cut with hand pressure only, if possible; otherwise, tap the chisel lightly with the mallet. Cut alternately across and down the grain until you have cleared all the waste out of the sockets. Then assemble the joint as described in Step 7, opposite.

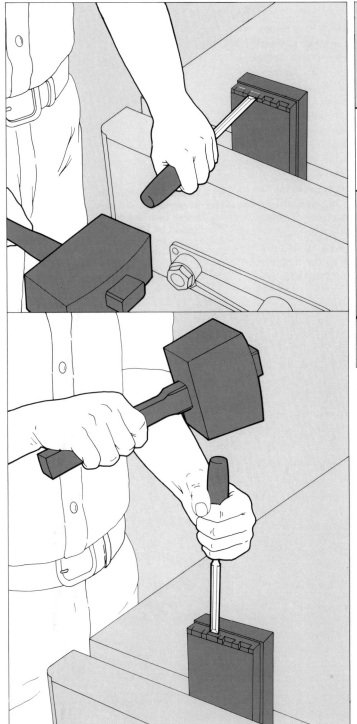

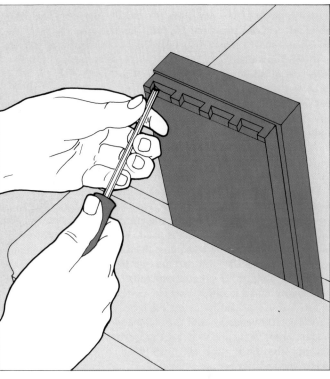

Dovetails Made by the Dozen

For projects that require large numbers of dovetail joints, a time-saving alternative to cutting them by hand (*page 44*) is offered by a special device known as a dovetail jig, used in conjunction with a router to cut both sides of a simple dovetail joint simultaneously. A simpler, cheaper jig for use with a high-speed power drill is also available, but with this sockets and tails must be cut in separate operations (*page 53*).

In machine-made dovetails the pins and tails are of uniform size; this makes the joint a little less decorative than a hand-cut one but, since the fit is very accurate, the strength of the joint is not significantly reduced. However, only lap dovetails can be made with the jig because it produces tails with rounded ends which remain hidden inside a lap joint.

Despite its complicated appearance, the dovetail jig is quite simple to use. The two boards to be joined are held by the cramp bars against the top and side of the metal base, and the jig is lowered against them to guide the router. Moving in and out between the tongues, the router cuts tails in one board and matching sockets in the other. Care is needed to mount the boards in the correct sequence and the right way up but, once the jig and router are properly set up, the work proceeds quickly and easily corner after corner.

The best way to set the device up is to cut a test joint in scrap wood the same thickness and width as the two pieces to be joined. The test joint should fit snugly, the two pieces meeting flush at the corners and the tails completely seated in the sockets. If the joint is too loose, you can correct it by slightly increasing the depth setting of the router. If the joint is too tight to fit together when tapped lightly with a mallet, decrease the router's depth setting. If the tails fall above or below the surface of the sockets, adjust the position of the jig: for sockets that are too shallow, move the jig backwards by turning the adjusting nuts clockwise; for sockets that are too deep, turn the adjusting nuts anticlockwise, bringing the jig forwards.

The orientation of the router during the cut can also affect the depth and snugness of the joint. While you are cutting test joints, note the position of the router handles in relation to the work; when you achieve a good fit, make all subsequent cuts with the router handles in this position. When the test joint is perfect, do not change the adjustments until you have finished cutting all the dovetails. Do not discard the test joint, however, because if you plan to repeat joints of the same dimensions later you can use it to reset the bit depth on the router.

By changing the size of the router bit and the jig bar, you can make dovetails of several sizes. The most common dovetails are 25 mm or 12 mm wide across the widest part of the tail. Broader ones are generally used for drawers and cabinets, and narrower ones for small boxes.

Whatever the size of the dovetails, the cutting positions for making the joint are always the same. The tail piece is always vertical against the front of the base, the socket piece horizontal against the top of the base. If the finished joint will be exposed, you can improve its appearance by planning the total width of the joint so that it begins and ends on a half pin: make the final tail half as wide as the distance between the tips of the jig tongues.

A machine-made flush dovetail joint. When assembled, the tail and socket pieces of a router-cut dovetail joint look much like those of a hand-cut dovetail except that the tails and pins are identical in size. The hidden ends of the tails and sockets are rounded, however, and the tail cuts in the socket piece usually do not extend through the wood's full thickness (*inset*).

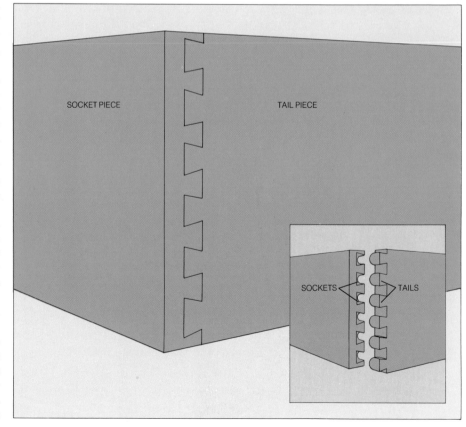

SOCKET PIECE

TAIL PIECE

SOCKETS TAILS

Assembling the Jig and Router

Setting up a jig and router. A dovetail jig device *(below, left)* and a specially fitted router *(below, right)* together make short work of cutting the two parts of an interlocking dovetail joint. The jig device is shown here mounted on a 225 by 50 mm board clamped to the top of a worktable, but it could be mounted directly on the work surface. The device consists of a channel-shaped base, above which lies the actual jig. Two knobs, one on each jig bracket, adjust the jig's height, and two nuts behind the brackets *(inset)* move the jig forwards or backwards for fine tuning.

The two boards being cut are held by bar cramps against the top and front of the base; on most models, the cramps can be adjusted so that they will take boards up to 330 mm wide and 30 mm thick. The boards are butted against stop pegs on the top and front of the base; the pegs are offset to the precise distance required to bring the finished joint into alignment. The router base is fitted with a guide bushing that follows the exact contours of the jig, and the special dovetail bit is tapered so that it will cut precisely angled tails and sockets.

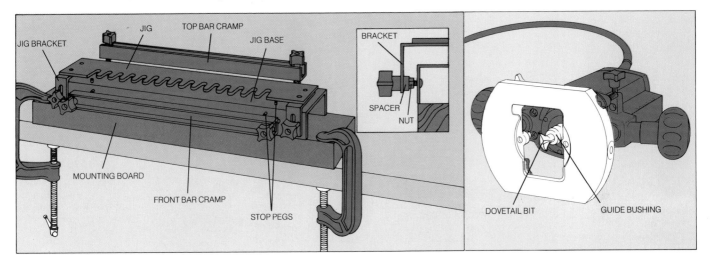

Routing to Make a Flush Dovetail

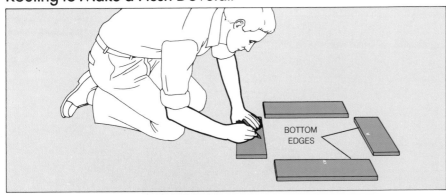

1 Marking the pieces. Lay the pieces on a flat surface in the order they will assume when assembled, their bottom edges towards each other and their inside faces up. Mark the front piece with the letter A, then mark the remaining pieces B, C and D, moving clockwise. Place each mark near the bottom edge of the board, to help orientate each piece in the dovetail jig. The bottom edges will always butt against the stop pegs and the inside faces will always face away from the base of the jig.

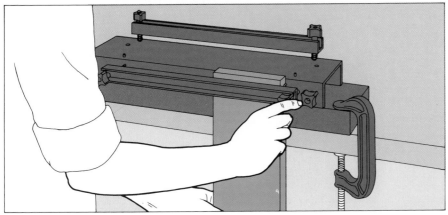

2 Setting up the first piece. Place the side piece marked D inside the front bar cramp at the right side of the jig base, with its bottom edge against the stop peg. Slide the piece up until its end is about 6 mm above the surface of the jig base. Tighten the front bar cramp.

3 **Setting up the second piece.** Slide the front piece, marked A, under the top bar cramp at the right side of the jig base, bottom edge against the stop peg and end butted squarely against the side of piece D. Tighten the top bar cramp. Then loosen the front bar cramp slightly, and slide piece D up until its end is flush with the top surface of piece A. Lower the jig over the two pieces, and fasten it securely in position with the locking knobs on the base *(inset)*.

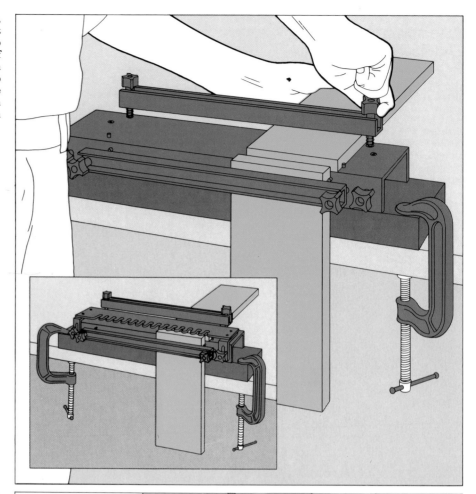

4 **Routing the outer edge.** Depress the router bit and lock it in position. Beginning at the right side of the jig base, position the guide bushing of the router against the slotted jig; switch on the router, and begin moving it from right to left. Move the router straight across the edge of the piece held by the front cramp, touching each tongue of the slotted jig with the guide bushing as the router passes it.

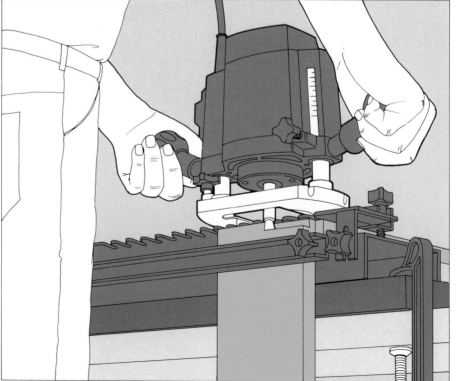

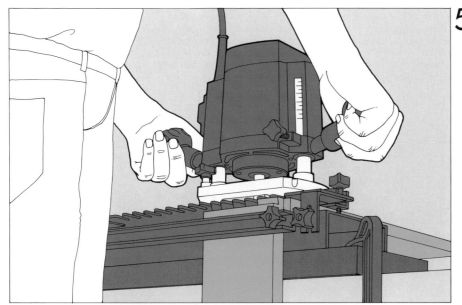

5 **Completing the joint.** Starting at the left side of the two pieces, move the router slowly to the right, using the guide bushing to follow the contours of the jig tongues. When the cut is complete, switch off the router and allow it to come to a stop; then withdraw the router from the jig, pulling it directly towards you. Remove the two pieces from the fixture, and clean away any splinters around the tails and sockets with a trimming knife.

Cut the other side of the front piece, marked A, in the same way, matching it with the side piece marked B, but for this cut clamp the assembly against the left side of the jig base. Repeat the same procedures with the back piece, marked C, and with the uncut ends of the two side pieces. Assemble the joints as you would hand-cut dovetails *(page 48, Step 7)*.

Dovetailing with a Drill

Using a simple jig. Mark the insides of the boards in which the sockets and tails will be cut. Secure the dovetail bit, cutter guide and connector to the drill. Slide the cutter guide into a slot in the grid and adjust its position to correspond to the thickness of the tail piece, then secure the depth stop with its locknut. Clamp the socket piece and grid to the edge of the workbench. Holding the dovetailer handle with your left hand, drill through the slots to cut out the sockets *(left)*.

Mark off the position of one of the sockets on the edge of the tail piece, then place the tail piece on a scrap timber on the workbench and clamp the grid in position. Holding the drill horizontally and, cutting from the top edge of the board down into the scrap timber, cut out the tails. Clean out any splinters round the sockets and tails, then assemble the joint.

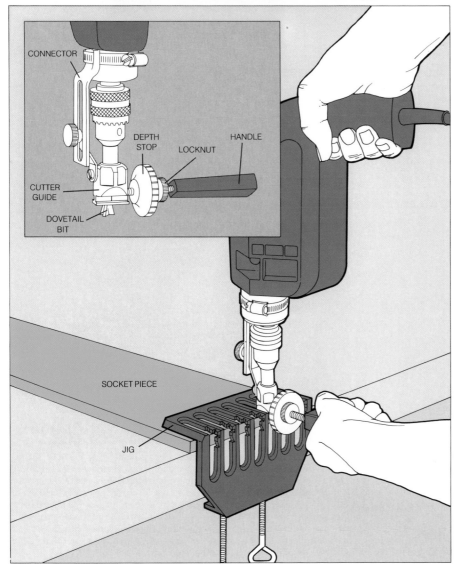

The Comb Joint— Fast and Strong

The comb or box joint, widely used in the cheap pine produce boxes of yesteryear, is still very useful to the woodworker of today, for drawers as well as boxes. Its straight-sided fingers and slots are quickly cut by machine and, although not inter-locking like the angled tails and pins of the dovetail, they provide a large gluing area that makes the joint very strong.

Comb joints can be cut on a table saw using a simple jig attached to the mitre fence. Many manufacturers offer an ad-justable comb-joint jig as an accessory, but they are not difficult to make. Accurate construction is essential to make the joint fit, however, and the jig should be tested on scrap wood. Also, the joint should be planned so that a complete finger falls at each end of the joint. The easiest way to do this is to adjust the height of your box or drawer according to the width of the blade you are using.

A wide saw kerf is needed to cut the slots for this joint. This can be obtained by using a special blade known as a "wobbler": by means of an arrangement of adjustable washers, the blade is tilted on its axis and cuts a wide kerf as it spins. You can also use a special cluster of blades called a dado headset: and it is even possible to make a comb joint by making two or three passes with a carbide-tipped blade, which cuts a wider kerf than a standard crosscut blade. Making a comb joint on a table saw re-quires the removal of the crown guard and, if using a wobbler or a dado headset, of the riving knife as well. Exercise great care, and replace the knife and guard as soon as the job is finished.

The blade should be set to cut about 1 mm higher than the thickness of the wood. A cut of this depth will produce a joint whose fingers protrude slightly above the surface of the adjoining piece, but the unevenness is planed away after the glue has dried completely.

When you have cut all four corners, glue and assemble the joints and clamp each corner in both directions, using small bar cramps. If you use blocks of scrap wood to prevent the wood surface from being marked by the cramps, cut a rebate in the part of each block that laps over the slightly protruding fingers.

A comb joint and its jig. Square-cut fingers and slots on the ends of matching boards mesh to form a comb joint *(below, left)*. The slots, which are spaced evenly to leave fingers of the same width, are cut with the aid of a special jig *(below, right)* attached to the mitre gauge of a table saw.

The jig used when making these joints is a piece of 18 mm plywood, measuring 100 mm high and about 450 mm long. A hardwood guide pin is attached to the front of the jig. First a slot is cut in the jig with the saw blade, and then the guide pin is cut so that it fits exactly into the slot.

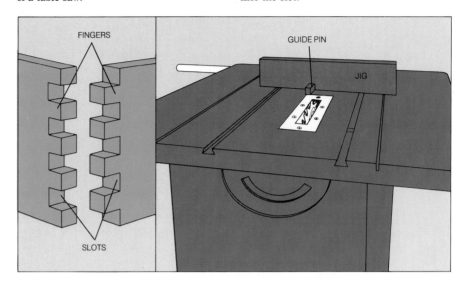

Cutting Serrated Edges with a Wobbler

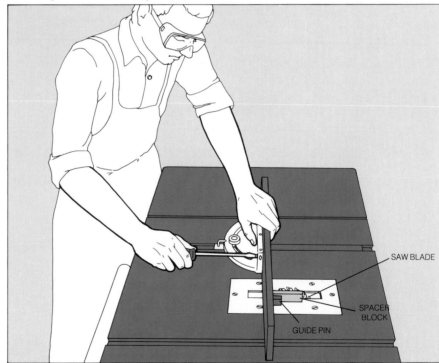

1 Setting up the jig. Switch on the saw and, hold-ing the jig firmly against the mitre gauge, slide the mitre gauge forward to cut a slot in the jig. Switch the saw off. Fit the hardwood guide pin into the slot and fasten it with a countersunk screw driven in from underneath. To position the jig, rotate the blade by hand until the part of the blade which spins furthest to the right (as you face the machine) is level with the table at the front of the blade slot. Holding the jig against the mitre gauge, move it forward until it is almost touching the saw teeth. Then put a wooden spacer block, of the same thickness as the guide pin, against the saw blade, and move the jig sideways until the guide pin presses the block against the saw blade. With the jig held in this position, attach it to the mitre gauge using wood screws *(above)*.

2 **Making the first slot.** Hold the inside face of the first board firmly against the jig, with one long edge butted against the guide pin. Switch on the saw, and push the jig and board slowly across the blade, cutting a slot through both the board and the jig. Switch off the saw. Wait for the saw to stop, and then return the jig to its starting position.

3 **Cutting the remaining slots.** Reposition the board by slipping the first slot *(Step 2)* over the guide pin. Hold the board firmly against the jig, and cut another slot. Cut each subsequent slot by repositioning each newly cut slot over the guide pin in the same manner.

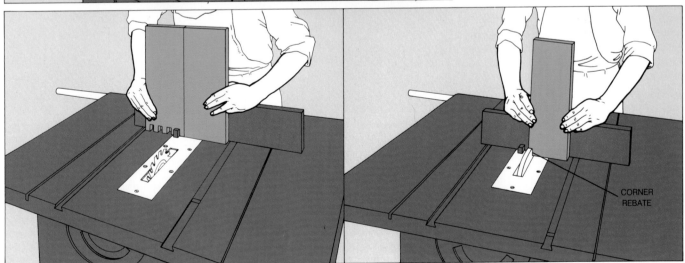

CORNER
REBATE

4 **Cutting the matching board.** Position the first board so that its outside face is against the jig and the first slot fits over the guide pin. Butt the matching board up against it, putting the inside face against the jig *(above, left)*. Hold the matching board firmly against the jig, and remove the first board. Then push the matching board across the blade, so that a rebate is cut at the corner *(above, right)*. Slip the rebate over the guide pin and continue cutting additional slots across the board, as in Step 3, ending with a rebate in the opposite corner.

Mortise and Tenon: Elements of a Strong Joint

Mortise and tenon joinery is based on a simple premise: hollow out a space in one piece, and shape a projection on a second piece to fit into it. The connection, as well as being simple, is strong—especially for joints where pressure will be applied perpendicular to the narrow edge of the second piece. It is often found in furniture parts that have cross rails, such as table or chair legs—the legs will have the hollowed-out spaces, called mortises, and the cross rails have the projections, called tenons. Variations of this joint bind the frames of many cabinet doors and window frames.

The general rule in planning a mortise and tenon joint is to make the tenon between one-third and one-half the thickness of the piece from which it projects. A tenon thinner than one-third the thickness is likely to be weak, while a tenon wider than half the thickness of the piece may leave the mortise sides too thin. Usually, vertical frame members contain the mortise, and horizontal members have the tenon.

Although in the planning stage the size of the tenon is considered first, in execution it is the mortise that leads: if any mistake is made in fashioning the mortise, the tenon can still be shaped to fit. Mortises can be scooped out with a chisel, but power tools make neater holes with less effort. Similarly, tenons can be fashioned with a dovetail saw; but faster, cleaner cuts can be made with a band saw or by making repeated passes with a table saw *(page 59)*. If you need to make a large number of identical joints, a spindle moulder can be used to make the tenons, and a mortising machine, such as is found on many combination machines, to cut out the mortises.

In professional workshops, mortises are sometimes hollowed out with a drill press fitted with a mortiser, which has a regular drill bit sheathed in a square cutter. The bit drills a round hole; the cutter trims it to make it square. A more common accessory in home workshops is the drill stand *(opposite page)*, which enables you to cut accurate holes perpendicular to the board edge with an ordinary power drill. The rounded mortise left by the drill bit must be squared with a chisel. Although squaring the mortise in this way is standard practice, some woodworkers find it easier and faster to round the ends of the tenon with a rasp or file instead.

Boards too long to be clamped to a drill-stand base can be mortised with a router. The tool's high-speed cutting action leaves clean sides and a hole that needs less chiselling than drilled holes.

A joint similar to the mortise and tenon joint, and one also used for the frames of furniture and cabinets, is the lap joint. Both of the adjoining pieces have projecting ends, like tenons, but the cutaway portions are formed in the course of shaping the projections. Lap-joint pieces are cut with the techniques used for tenons.

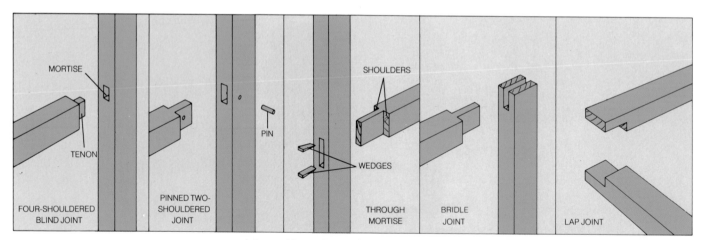

Joinery with mortises and tenons. Mortise and tenon joints can take several forms, varying in appearance and strength. When the mortise does not extend through the piece from one side to the other, the joint is called blind. The blind joint shown is called four-shouldered because the tenon is recessed at the top and bottom and on the two sides, or cheeks, so that four shoulders are formed. This joint is useful when one or both pieces are to be carved, since the shoulders can be whittled without exposing the mortise or the tenon. Uncarved, the broad shoulders are useful for covering any scratches or mistakes made in cutting the mortise.

The two-shouldered mortise is slightly stronger than its four-shouldered cousin because its tenon is larger, offering a greater gluing surface. The one shown here is additionally strengthened by a dowel and is called a pinned joint. Any mortise and tenon joint can be pinned for added strength. The through mortise has a mortise that penetrates to the far side of the mortise piece and exposes the end grain of the tenon; the joint is decorative when done in tables or chairs and is particularly useful in narrow wood, where a mortise cut only part way through does not provide for a deep enough tenon. The through mortise shown here has splayed ends to accept thin wedges, which strengthen the joint. The bridle joint, often known as an open mortise joint, is used at the corners of many frame constructions. The lap joint, which consists of two lapped tenons and no mortise at all, is used for joining the pieces of cabinet-frame fronts.

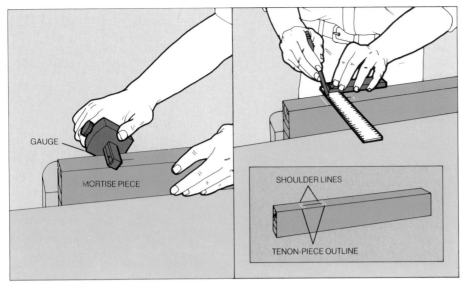

Marking Wood for a Mortise

Scribing the drilling line. Set the pin of a marking gauge at the approximate centre of the edge of the board; then press the pin into the board, leaving a mark. Rest the gauge against the other side of the board, and make a mark. Repeat these measurements, adjusting the pin until the two marks overlap—this indicates that you have located the exact centre of the edge. Draw the gauge down the board, scribing a line slightly shorter than the length of the mortise.

Butt the tenon piece against the marked edge of the mortise piece, and outline where its edges fall. For a four-shouldered joint, measure in from these two lines, and use a try square to mark top and bottom shoulders of equal width on the mortise edge (*near left*).

Cutting a Mortise on a Drill Stand

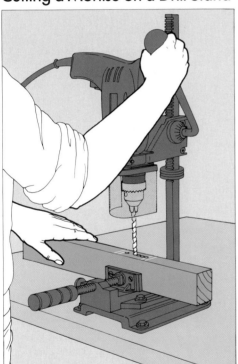

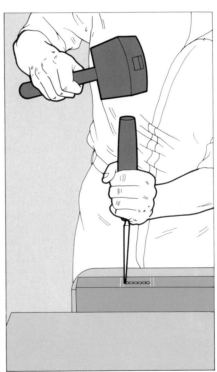

Drill Stand Safety Rules

To ensure safety, accuracy and stability when using a power drill secured in a drill stand, observe the following rules:

☐ Bolt the base of the drill stand securely on to a sturdy workbench.

☐ Clamp the stock firmly in position before you begin drilling.

☐ When making a deep hole, raise the bit frequently to clean out fragments of waste wood.

☐ Always keep the drill-stand base and the workbench clean.

☐ Make sure that the bit is fully tightened in the chuck, and that the chuck key is removed after tightening.

☐ Turn off the drill if the bit begins to bind.

1 Drilling out the cavity. With the drill firmly secured in the drill stand and fitted with a bit to match the width of the planned mortise, bore a row of holes down the scribed line. To adjust the drill, first mark the planned depth of the mortise on the board face and lower the cutting edge of the bit to that line; lock the depth stop. To adjust the mortise piece, move it until the drill tip falls exactly over the mortise line; clamp the board firmly in the drill-stand vice.

Drill a hole at one end of the mortise line, just inside the shoulder line, and a similar hole at the other end. Then drill holes in between, overlapping adjacent holes slightly.

2 Squaring the mortise with a chisel. Clamp the mortise piece in a vice, and use a marking gauge to scribe lines along both sides of the row of holes. At one end of the mortise, position a chisel that has a blade the same width as the mortise. Holding the shaft of the chisel exactly perpendicular, bevel facing the row of holes, tap the chisel with a mallet, squaring the end of the mortise. Repeat this procedure at the other end of the mortise.

Smooth each side of the mortise in the same fashion, positioning the chisel blade so that the bevelled edge faces the holes and the chisel shaft so that the cut will be straight down.

Using a Router
to Make a Mortise

1 **Setting up the router guide.** Install a straight bit with a diameter at least half the planned mortise width, and slide a fence guide on to one side of the router. Make the distance between the fence and the bit equal to the width of the planned tenon shoulder; lock the fence in place.

Adjust the router bit to the desired depth of cut, and make a test cut on a piece of scrap wood to check the width of the shoulder. Adjust the bit again, as necessary, before proceeding to cut the actual mortise piece.

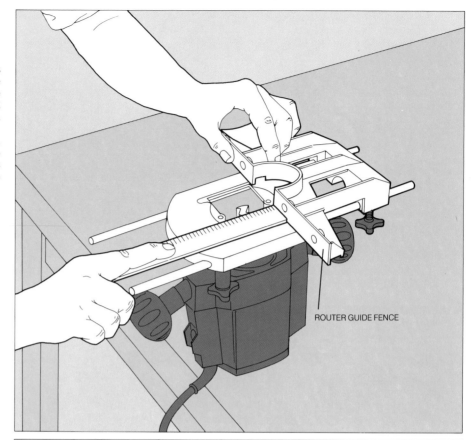

ROUTER GUIDE FENCE

2 **Making the cuts.** To support the router base, clamp a wide block of scrap wood alongside the mortise piece in a vice, the top of the block flush with the surface to be mortised. Butt the guide fence against the mortise piece with the router base resting on the scrap block. Switch on the machine and lower the bit into the board, slightly inside one end of the mortise marks. Move the router down to the other end of the mortise and back, cutting a groove that barely touches both ends of the mortise. Raise the bit and turn off the router. Turn the board round and rout the other side of the mortise. Square the ends with a chisel as shown on page 57, Step 2.

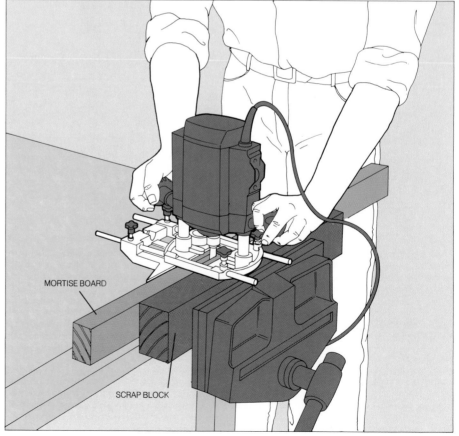

MORTISE BOARD

SCRAP BLOCK

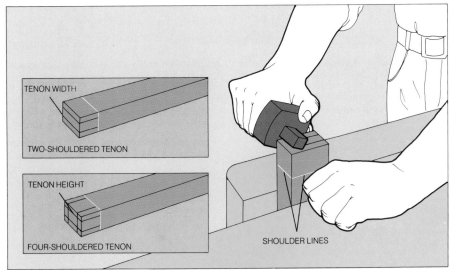

TENON WIDTH

TWO-SHOULDERED TENON

TENON HEIGHT

FOUR-SHOULDERED TENON

SHOULDER LINES

Shaping the Shoulders of a Matching Tenon

1 Marking the cutting lines. With a try square, draw a continuous line round all four sides of the tenon piece, marking the tenon shoulders. Make the tenon slightly shorter than the depth of the mortise. Using a mortise gauge, scribe lines on the end of the tenon piece to mark the width of the tenon, making it the same width as the mortise. Continue these lines down the edge of the board until they meet the shoulder lines (left, top inset). If the tenon is to have four shoulders, mark its height by scribing two additional lines, and extend them down to meet the shoulder lines (left, bottom inset).

2 Adjusting the saw-blade height. Install a crosscut carbide-tipped blade on the table saw and raise the head to a height roughly equal to the width of the tenon shoulder. Then lower it by a half turn of the blade-height crank. Using the mitre gauge as a guide, cut a rebate slightly less than the thickness of the mortise shoulder in one side of the tenon; then turn the board over and do the same on the other side. Test the tenon against the mortise. If they do not fit, raise the blade height very slightly and repeat the two cuts until tenon and mortise size match. Keep the blade at this height for the remainder of the tenon cuts.

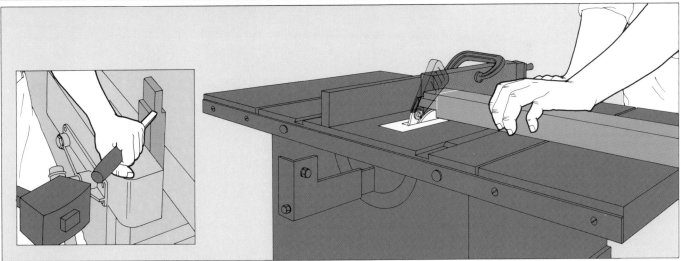

3 Completing the tenon cut. Clamp a wooden block to the rip fence, to use as a depth guide in cutting the tenon shoulder. Make the block long enough to extend from the near end of the fence to a point just short of where the tips of the carbide-tipped blade will start to cut. Move the fence and the wooden block towards the blade until the distance between the block and the blade edge furthest from the fence is equal to the distance from the shoulder line to the end of the tenon. Lock the fence. Butt the end of the tenon board against the block and, pushing with the mitre gauge, cut the shoulder. Bring the board back to the starting point and move it away from the block, so that the next pass will remove an uncut section of wood between the shoulder and the end of the tenon. Continue until the entire tenon side is exposed. Then turn the board over, and repeat these cuts to remove the wood from the other side of the mortise. The fit which is achieved should be snug, but not so tight that the grain on the tenon cheeks is compressed.

For a four-shouldered tenon, use the same technique, but cut shoulders on all four sides of the tenon board. If you have left the ends of the mortise curved rather than squaring them off, round the corners of the tenon as well. To do this, clamp the tenon board in a woodworking vice, and chip off the corners with a chisel held flat side down (inset). Then hold the chisel in a vertical position, bevel side out, and pare down the sharp corners. Smooth and round the corners with a rasp and a piece of sandpaper.

Pinning a Mortise and Tenon with a Dowel

1 **Drilling the dowel hole.** Fit a piece of scrap wood, roughly the same thickness as the tenon, into the empty mortise. Install a bit of the desired dowel diameter in a drill secured in a stand, and set the depth gauge so that it will stop the tip of the bit when it has passed through one side of the mor-

tise and has penetrated at least half way into the other side. Position the bit above the mid-point of the mortise, slightly closer to the front edge; then drill the hole for the dowel. The piece of scrap wood will prevent the mortise wall from splintering as you drill.

Discard the scrap wood, and insert the tenon in the mortise. Lay both on a worktable, and push a drill bit—the one just used or one of identical size—through the dowel hole until its tip has marked the tenon (*inset*). Remove the bit from the hole, and the tenon from the mortise.

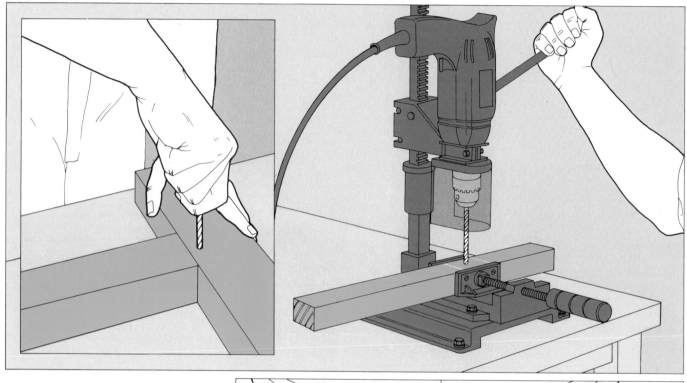

2 **Shifting the hole mark.** To draw the shoulders tight, make a pencil mark on the tenon about a thumbnail's thickness away from the impression made by the drill-bit tip, in towards the shoulder. Drill a hole in the tenon, identical in size to the one in the mortise, using the second mark as the centre. Cut a dowel the same diameter as the hole and 6 mm longer; chamfer its end.

Spread glue in the mortise and on both the end and the shoulders of the tenon, and fit the pieces together. Spread glue in the dowel hole and on the chamfered end of the dowel, and tap the dowel into the hole. Let the glue set for a day, then trim the dowel flush with the face of the mortise board, using a dovetail saw; finally, sand the dowel end smooth.

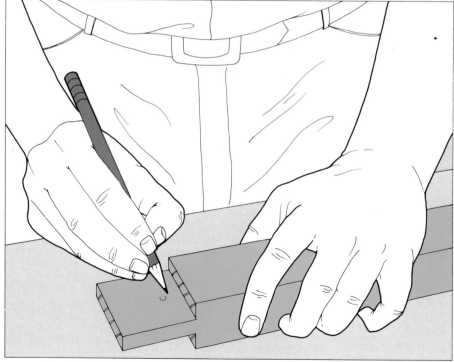

Two Joints with an Open Mortise

Making a bridle joint. Scribe drilling lines on opposite sides of the board to be mortised about 50 mm in from the end. Using a drill secured in a stand, drill a series of holes to a depth of just over half the width of the board *(page 57)*, then turn the board over and drill through from the opposite side. Square out the through mortise with a chisel, and cut the tenon piece *(page 59)*.

Glue and assemble the joint. If the boards are part of a frame construction, assemble and glue the other joints and secure cramps across the frame on either side of the joints *(below)*. When the glue has dried, saw off the waste wood to the side of each joint so that you expose the edge of the tenons *(inset)*.

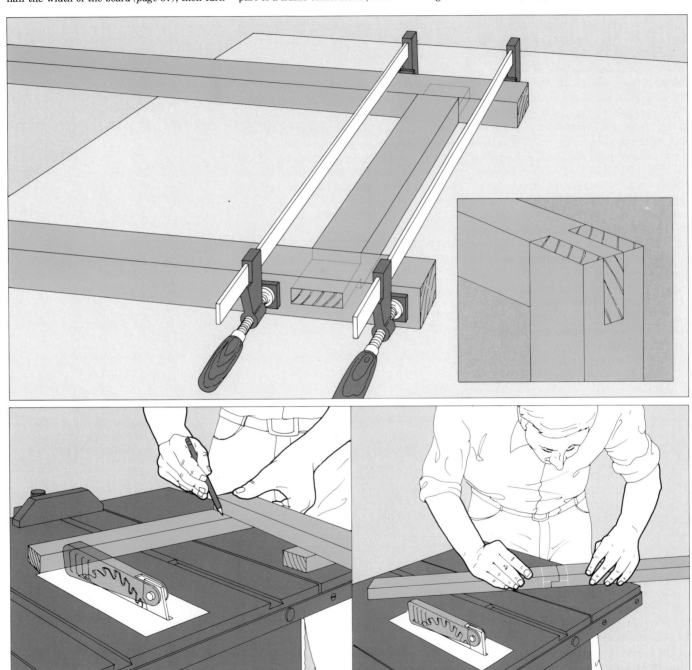

Spliced ends for lap joints. Lap the ends of the pieces to be joined over each other at a right angle, and mark shoulder lines on the adjoining faces *(above, left)*. Use a try square to continue the lines around each board, then add a line along the middle of each edge to extend from the shoulder line to the end.

Secure a carbide-tipped blade in a table saw. Raise the blade so that its height is equal to the width of the shoulder—half the thickness of the piece of wood—and then lower it by a half turn of the blade-height crank. Make test cuts at the end of each piece, and then fit the two ends together *(above, right)*; take note of how much deeper the cut needs to be in order to make the pieces flush with each other. Raise the blade by small degrees, continuing to make test cuts and to test the fit after each pair of cuts. When the two pieces fit together perfectly, cut away the rest of the wood, back as far as the shoulder lines, as described on page 59, Step 3.

Using Dowels to Lock Joints

A blind dowel joint is a kind of lazy man's mortise and tenon joint. The parts are connected, without needing to be shaped, by hidden wooden pegs. Dowel joints are quicker and easier to cut than mortise and tenon joints. They are not quite so strong, but are sturdy enough to be used in many tables, chairs and cabinet frames.

To make a proper joint, the diameter of the dowel should be one-third to one-half the thickness of the wood it enters. It should project at least 15 mm into each side of the joint, and its length should be 4 mm shorter than the combined depth of the two holes into which it fits. In addition, a dowel joint should consist of at least two dowels, since a single dowel will have little resistance to twisting.

The holes must be exactly perpendicular to the board edges into which they are drilled, and all matching holes must be perfectly aligned. Such precision is best achieved on a horizontal boring machine. Some pillar drills are fitted with tables that can be tilted into a true vertical position and used for boring into the ends of boards. For those who do not own such machines, however, a dowelling jig, used in conjunction with a portable drill, offers a suitable alternative. The function of dowelling—which is available in various designs—is to hold a drill-bit guide at a true right angle over the edge of a board. The bit of a portable drill is then inserted in the guide to bore the hole.

Another hole-alignment method uses dowel centres—metal pegs with a sharp point at one end. After the holes have been drilled in one board, a dowel centre is inserted, point out, into each hole. The joining piece is then pressed in place against them, and the points mark where the matching holes are to be drilled.

After the holes are made, glue is spread on the ends of the dowels and the sides of the holes; then the dowels are inserted. The dowels, which should be the same diameter as the holes, fit so snugly that they tend to trap air and excess glue in the bottom of the hole. If this happens, the dowels will not penetrate the proper distance. Pressure applied during clamping may force the dowels down, but in the process it may also crack one of the joint pieces.

To prevent air and glue from interfering with the seating of the dowels, escape routes should be provided. You can buy pre-cut dowels, with straight or spiralling grooves, at hardware shops and timber merchants, or you can groove the dowels yourself. This can be done by knocking the dowels through a purchased dowel sizer with serrated-edge holes, or by cutting grooves using a fine-toothed saw. If you are in a hurry, you can even groove dowels by pulling the serrated jaws of pliers down their length, impressing them with furrows. Finally, to ease the entry of the dowels, you can chamfer their ends with a rasp or sandpaper, or alternatively with a special tool called a dowel rounder. The latter works like a pencil sharpener and can be fitted into a drill.

Drilling Holes for a Blind Dowel Joint

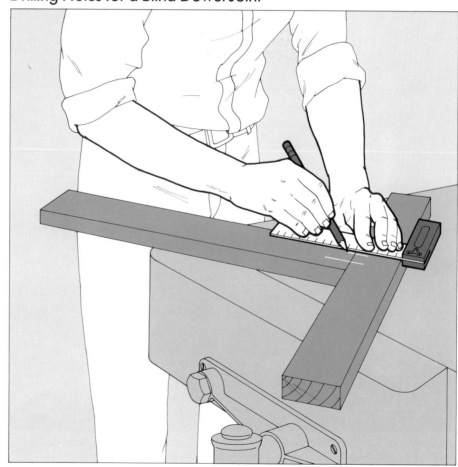

1 **Marking the dowel locations.** Take the two pieces to be joined and place them face-side up on a worktable, aligned in their finished position. Then, using a try square, mark a line for each dowel across both boards.

2 **Boring the holes.** Fit a bit guide of the required size to a dowelling jig, and clamp the jig to one board edge, aligning the jig centre line with one of the pencil lines made in Step 1 *(below, left)*. Then align the centre of the bit guide with the exact centre of the board edge. (In the jig shown here, this is achieved by using numerical scales and a thumbscrew to make the adjustment.) Fit the drill with the appropriate size bit, and add a depth gauge to stop the bit when it has reached the correct depth. Then drill the hole *(below, right)*. Reposition the dowelling jig to drill additional holes in the board edge. Then drill matching holes in the edge of the adjoining board.

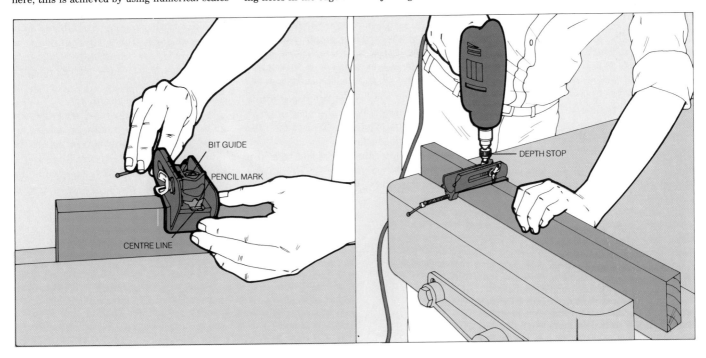

BIT GUIDE
PENCIL MARK
CENTRE LINE
DEPTH STOP

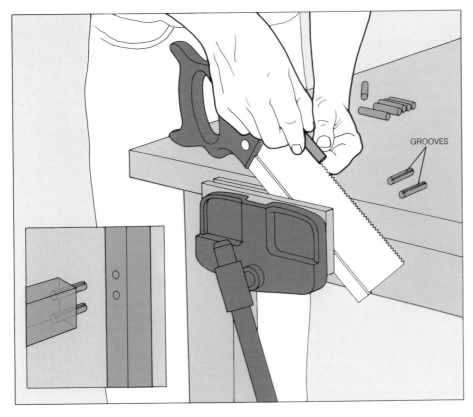

GROOVES

Preparing and Installing the Dowels

Grooving the dowels. Fasten a fine-toothed saw, such as a tenon saw or dovetail saw, in a vice with the teeth uppermost. Trim the dowels to size, then run each one carefully back and forth over the blade *(left)*. Cut at least two grooves in the dowel, one down each side. Chamfer the ends, and then spread glue in the holes and on the dowel ends. Insert the dowels into one of the pieces *(inset)*, join the pieces, clamp the joint and wipe away excess glue.

Mitre Joints Reinforced from Inside

A mitre joint, precisely cut, will give any corner a clean, finished appearance. In fact, it is the neatness and not the strength of this angled joint that keeps the mitre a favourite in the woodworker's repertoire, for the mitre is weak compared with other corner bonds. However, if strengthened with plywood splines *(below)*, most mitre joints have more than enough muscle to be able to hold their own against everyday use and abuse.

Common mitre joints are made by cutting 45-degree angles on two pieces of wood and joining the pieces to form a right-angled corner. There are two categories:

flat joints and edge joints. Flat mitres, cut across the face of the wood, are used mostly for decoration—to join the vertical and horizontal strips that cover the front edges of many cabinets, for example, especially those built of plywood. Picture frames, too, are almost always made with flat mitre joints. Edge mitres are made by cutting a bevel along each of the two edges which are to be joined. They are used in case construction—to join the four sides of a basic box-shaped cabinet.

Splines—thin slivers of wood that slip into grooves cut along the adjoining faces of both flat and edge mitre joints—are

commonly made from 3 mm plywood. If you use plywood of this thickness, the spline grooves can be quickly and accurately cut with a regular 3 mm blade on a spindle moulder. For a stronger joint in thicker wood, use an adjustable grooving blade to cut the grooves and 6 mm plywood to make the spline. Test-fit a spline joint before gluing it together.

Although almost any hand or power saw can be used to cut the mitres, the table saw is the tool most woodworkers prefer. It makes angled cuts easily and precisely, especially when used with the simple jig described on page 66.

Three mitre joints and splines. The three mitre joints shown here, all reinforced with splines, are appropriate—each in its own way—in many different woodworking situations. The diagonal-spline mitre is used for edge joints; the spline, set diagonal to the faces of the wood, runs the entire length of the joint. A triangular-spline mitre is used for the flat mitre joints found in frame construction; such a spline is set into the outside corner of the joint. A blind-spline mitre, used either in edge construction, as shown, or in frame construction, has a spline that is invisible on the outer edge of the joint; it combines strength with neat appearance.

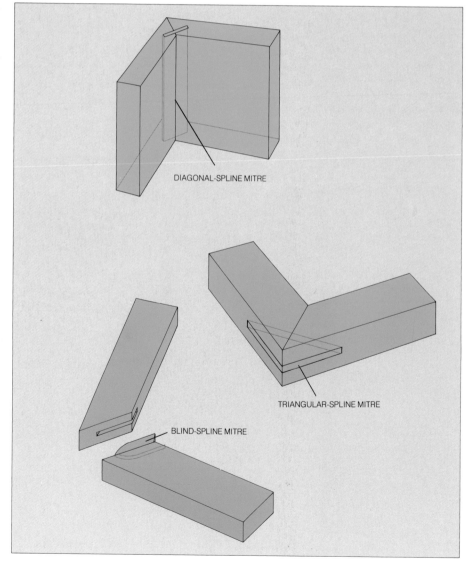

DIAGONAL-SPLINE MITRE

TRIANGULAR-SPLINE MITRE

BLIND-SPLINE MITRE

Setting a Diagonal Spline into a Mitred Edge

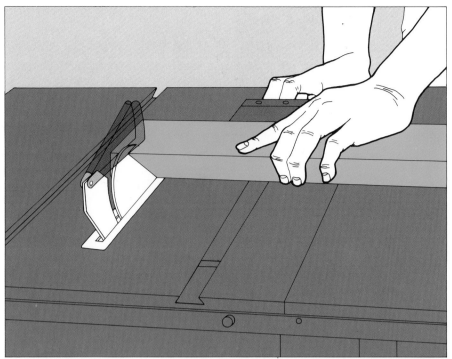

1 **Making the bevel cuts.** To bevel the ends of the boards on a table saw, set the blade at a 45-degree angle and set the mitre gauge at a 90-degree angle. Turn on the saw. With one hand holding the board flat against the table and firmly against the mitre gauge, push the mitre gauge forwards with the other hand, directing the end of the board through the blade. Then cut the second board; the top faces of the two boards will be on the outside of the joint.

To set up the saw for cutting the spline groove, lower the blade to a height of 9 mm, but leave it tilted at a 45-degree angle. Remove the blade guard and lower or remove the riving knife. Remove the mitre gauge from its channel, and install the rip fence so that the blade tilts away from it. Lay one cut board on the table, bevelled end against the fence and bevel facing down, and bring the fence towards the blade until the lower edge of the bevel is lined up with the edge of the saw slot; lock the fence in this position.

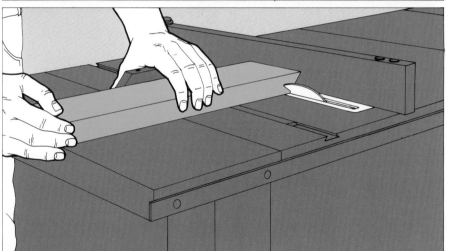

2 **Cutting grooves for the spline.** Hold the board firmly against the table with one hand and against the rip fence with the other while you push the board past the blade, cutting a groove into the bevelled surface 3 mm above its lower edge. Cut the second board in the same way. Return the blade to a vertical position, replace the blade guard and riving knife, then move the rip fence to the other side of the blade.

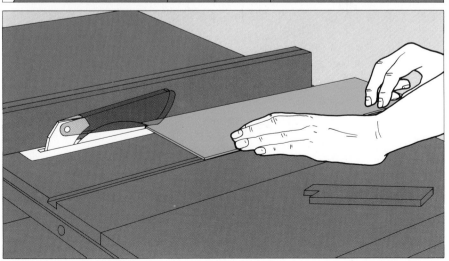

3 **Cutting the spline.** Cut the spline from 3 mm plywood. First butt a piece of plywood against the fence, and push it past the blade to obtain a strip 18 mm wide; use a push stick to protect your fingers as you approach the end of the cut. Then, using a mitre gauge instead of the fence, cut off a section of the plywood strip the same length as the bevelled edges of the joint.

4 **Assembling the joint.** Place the two boards on edge, bevel to bevel, on a flat surface. Coat both bevelled ends and both faces of the spline with PVA glue. Slip one spline edge into a groove, and then push the groove of the second board over the other edge of the spline. Press firmly, check the joint for alignment, then wipe away any excess glue and clamp the joint *(page 72)* until the glue has completely dried.

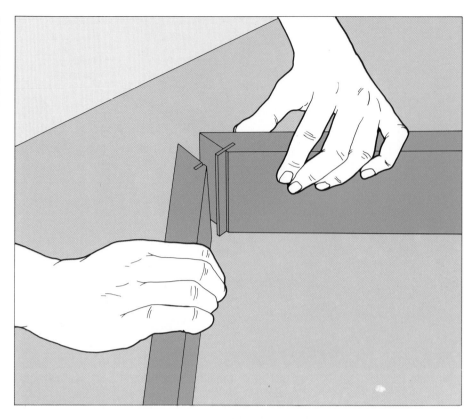

An Angled Jig for Cutting Flat Mitre Joints

Cutting multiple mitres. A mitre jig lets you cut a series of identical mitre joints on the table saw with a minimum of adjusting. Boards are held against the face of the angled mitre guide as the jig is pushed past the blade; to cut the mitres in the other ends of the boards, the jig is simply slotted into the channel on the opposite side of the saw blade.

The base of the jig, which slides across the table on a runner that fits in the mitre-gauge channels, is a rectangle of 12 mm plywood; the width of the base is exactly twice the distance between the blade and the centre of the channel. The mitre guide, made of 50 by 25 mm hardwood, is screwed to the base at an angle of 45 degrees; its front end is about 150 mm from the edge of the base. A strip of sandpaper may be glued to the face of the guide to keep the boards from slipping as they are cut.

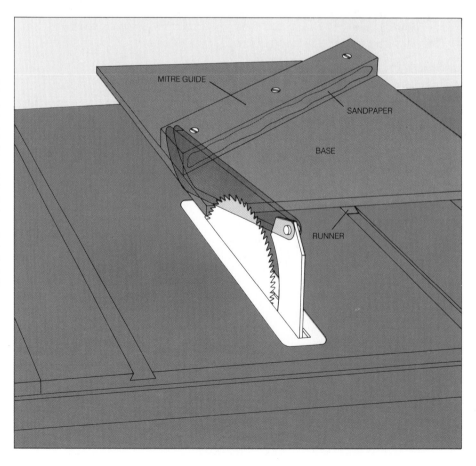

A Triangular Spline for a Mitred Corner

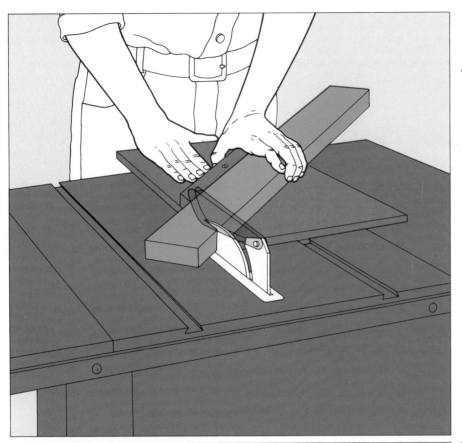

1 **Cutting and assembling the mitre joint.** Mark the location of the mitres on the edges of the boards to be joined, and position the mitring jig *(opposite page, below)* on the saw table. Then set a board on the jig, against a mitre guide, lining up the mark on the board with the centre slot. Turn on the saw and, holding the board firmly against the mitre guide, push the jig across the blade until the board is cut. Remove the jig from the saw table, slot its runner into the channel on the other side of the blade, and cut the second board in the same way. Apply glue to the joint and clamp it, using a corner cramp *(page 70)*.

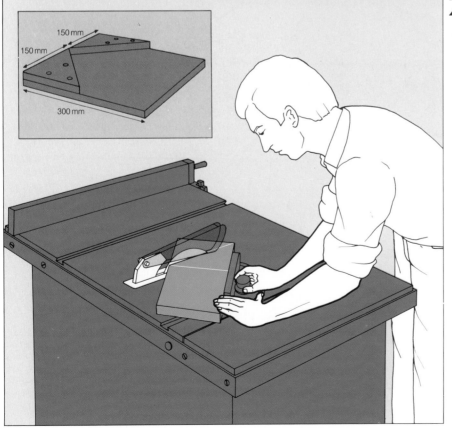

2 **Making a jig for the triangular groove.** On a piece of 150 by 300 mm timber the same thickness as the workpiece, mark off a 150 mm square. Using the mitre gauge on the table saw, cut across the square at a 45-degree angle *(left)*. Remove the gauge and cut off the waste section from the board to produce a second triangle. Align the triangular sections with the corners of a 300 mm square of 9 mm plywood, and screw and glue them in position.

3 **Cutting a triangular groove.** Set the corner of the glued mitre joint in the jig and place the jig on the worktable of a spindle moulder. Attach a 3 mm blade to the spindle and align the height of the blade with the centre of the joint. Secure a faceboard across the two halves of the fence, then switch on the machine and move the faceboard back until the blade protrudes to a depth just short of the centre of the mitre joint. Secure the fence by tightening the fence locking nuts. Lower the guard and test the accuracy of the blade setting with a piece of scrap timber. Pressing the joint against the jig with a square of wood on the inside of the joint, pass the joint-and-jig assembly through the machine to cut a 3 mm groove.

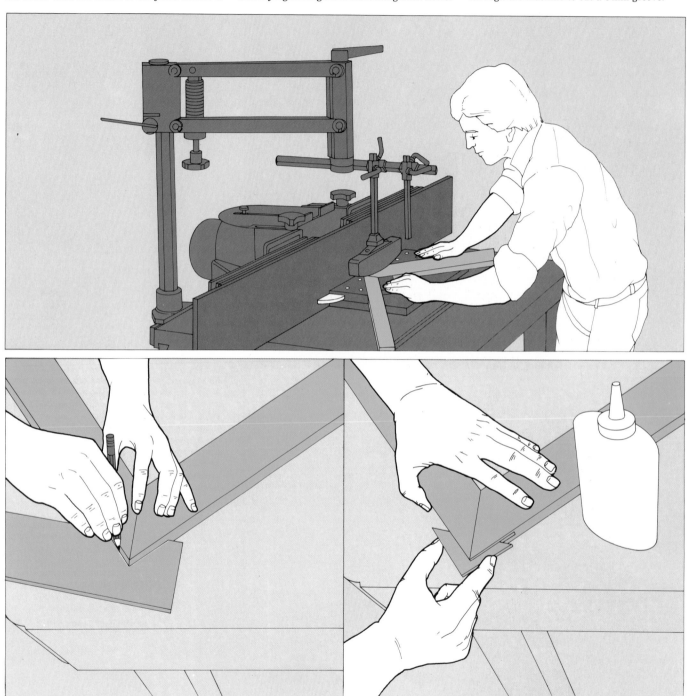

4 **Tracing and cutting a triangular spline.** Slide a piece of 3 mm plywood into the triangular groove you have cut, and outline the right angle formed by the outside edge of the joint *(above, left)*. Cut out the spline, spread glue on both sides and fit it into the groove *(above, right)*. Clamp the faces of the joint until the glue dries, then sand off protruding spline edges.

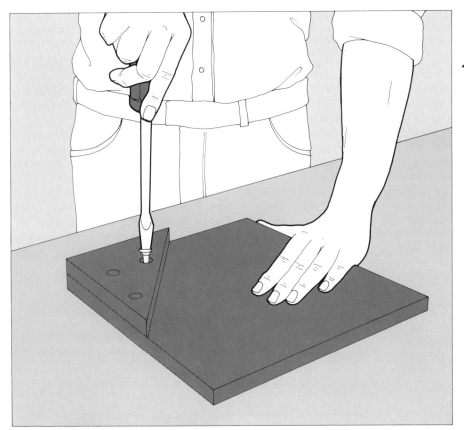

Cutting a Hidden Slot for a Blind Spline

1 **Making the jig.** Cut a 300 mm square base for the jig from 9 mm plywood. Cut a single triangle from a 150 by 150 mm piece of timber the same thickness as the workpiece *(page 67, Step 2)*; screw and glue the triangle to one corner of the base. Place one of the mitred boards to be joined on the base, with the inside of the joint against the triangle and the mitre in alignment with the front of the base.

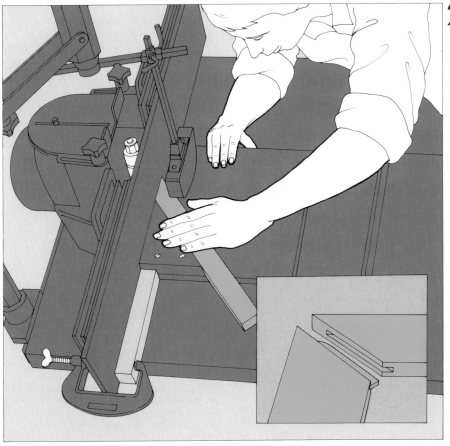

2 **Cutting grooves for the spline.** Adjust the blade on a spindle moulder to cut a groove 9 mm deep. Raise the blade and, looking down over the top of the machine, move the jig-and-joint assembly along the faceboard to a point where the blade will cut along three-quarters of the length of the mitred edge; clamp a scrap timber to the faceboard to act as a stop. Adjust the blade height to cut precisely in the centre of the board, then switch on the machine and push the joint-and-jig assembly along the faceboard to cut the groove. Cut a matching groove in the mitred edge of the second board in the same way.

Cut a rectangular spline from an 18 mm wide strip of 3 mm plywood, as long as the exposed edge of the grooves. Use a coping saw to trim the end of the spline into a tongue shape, matching the curve of the grooves. Test-fit the shape of the spline by assembling the joint without glue *(inset)*; when the spline fits, spread glue on the spline and the mitred ends, and clamp the joint together. After the glue is dry, use a coping saw to trim the end of the spline that protrudes from the inside corner of the joint.

Clamping Work of Varied Shapes and Sizes

Correct clamping is vital for a good glued joint. Pressure is needed both to help the glue penetrate the wood and to hold the joint pieces in position while the glue dries. But applying pressure is often more than a matter of turning a screw: the pressure must conform to the anatomy of the joint and to the contours of the surfaces being joined. You must choose the right cramp for the job; if you don't have the proper cramp, you must improvise one. For some joints, especially those involving irregular surfaces, you may have to fashion clamping aids from scrap wood.

The devices and techniques shown on the following pages solve the most common clamping problems. Some of the devices eliminate the need for cramps or reduce the number needed. Some call for specially shaped cauls—pieces of wood that fit between the cramps and the work being joined—to adapt odd shapes to the flat surfaces of standard cramp jaws.

The same basic principles apply to all of these methods of clamping, whether straightforward or inventive. First, the joint should be assembled without glue and tested for fit in the clamping apparatus.

Then, after the glue is applied and the joint is reassembled, pressure from the clamping should be applied evenly so that the pieces are not shifted out of alignment or out of square.

When the clamping involves several points of pressure, it is usually best to adjust centre cramps first, then work towards the ends, checking the alignment with a try square or a sliding bevel. And the pressure should be firm but not severe: excess force will squeeze so much glue into the wood pores that not enough will remain on the surfaces to act as a bond.

The Right Cramp for the Job

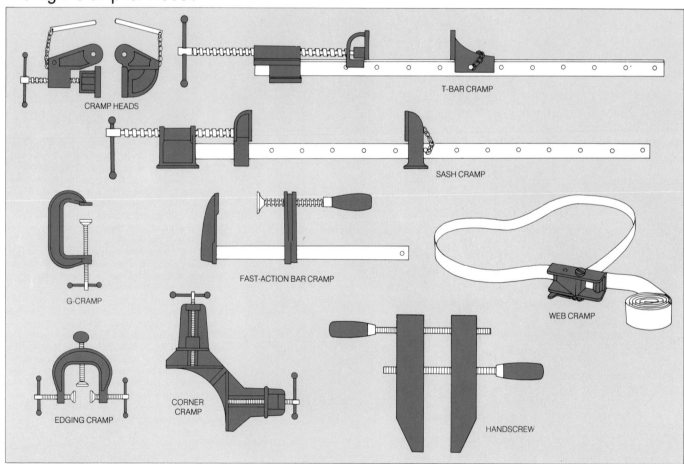

CRAMP HEADS

T-BAR CRAMP

SASH CRAMP

G-CRAMP

FAST-ACTION BAR CRAMP

WEB CRAMP

EDGING CRAMP

CORNER CRAMP

HANDSCREW

A catalogue of cramps. For large assemblies—edge-jointed panels, carcasses and frames—the bar or sash cramp is the tool of choice, being strong and quickly adjustable. The T-bar cramp is a heavy-duty version which will resist bending under pressure. Cramp heads, which are cheaper and more portable than a complete bar cramp, do the same job when they are fitted over a wooden rail of any length, 38 mm wide by 25 mm thick,

with holes drilled to accept the locating pins.

For smaller work, the G-cramp has long been a woodworker's stalwart: strong and versatile, it comes in a large choice of sizes. The more modern fast-action cramp has a wider span, but can be used in place of the G-cramp; the adjustable jaw slides freely along the bar and locks into position when the screw is tightened against the work. The advantage of the wooden-jawed handscrew, a

modern refinement of an age-old design, is that it can clamp non-parallel surfaces.

The jaws of a mitre or corner cramp apply pressure from two directions to clamp a right-angled joint. The centre spindle of an edging cramp presses edge moulding against the edge of a board gripped by the two opposing spindles. The web or band cramp, with its flexible strap, can hug the joints of large irregular structures.

Home-Made Substitutes
for Shop-Bought Cramps

An edging caul. The slightly concave edge of this long, narrow caul, clamped near the middle of two joined pieces—here, a shelf and its edge moulding—evenly distributes the pressure of just two cramps out to the ends of the pieces. The caul works equally well on pieces shorter than itself.

To make an edging caul, scribe a gentle arc on a 50 mm wide length of hardwood—oak, maple or birch—making the arc 6 mm higher at its midpoint than at its ends: the wood for the caul should be as thick as the width of the piece it will press. Cut the curve on a band saw, or use hand shaping tools (pages 84–85), and sand it smooth. Then place the concave edge (inset) against the work being glued, and apply the cramps. For cauls that are shorter than 600 mm, only one cramp will be necessary.

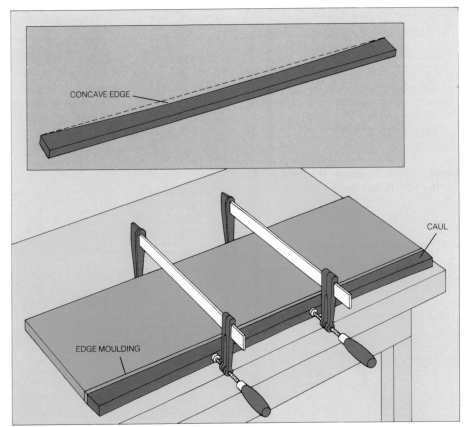

CONCAVE EDGE

CAUL

EDGE MOULDING

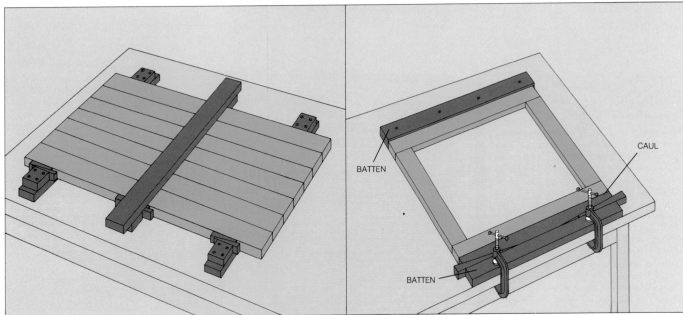

BATTEN

CAUL

BATTEN

Home-made bar cramps. If you do not own bar cramps, you can quite easily and satisfactorily duplicate their effect with either of the following techniques which use hardwood strips and wedges. In one method, you fabricate imitation bar cramps (above, left); in the alternative method, you force the far side of a joint against a wooden stop (above, right).

For the first method, shown here clamping board edges, begin by screwing square blocks to the ends of hardwood battens. Then place alternate battens on opposite faces of the joined boards, and gently drive wedges between the blocks and the board edges.

For the second method, first screw or clamp a batten to the worktable. Butt the far side of the joined pieces, here forming a cabinetry frame, against it. To the near side, add a hardwood caul, trimmed at the ends to accommodate wedges. Butt a second batten against the trimmed edge of the caul, and clamp the second batten firmly to the worktable. Then drive wedges as needed between the second batten and the caul.

When you are using either one of these substitute bar cramps, it is necessary to cut the wedges long and thin. A wedge measuring 100 mm in length should be no more than 2 mm wide at its large end and 6 mm at its small end. Make the wedges from hardwood if you intend to use them frequently.

One-of-a-Kind Cauls for Unique Situations

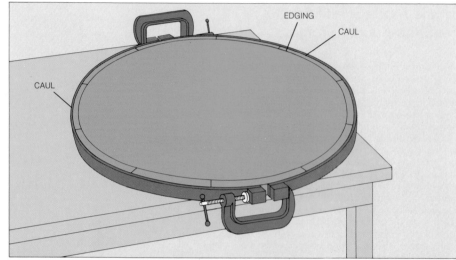

Cauls for curves. Held in position by two G-cramps, these two semicircular cauls distribute pressure around new tabletop edging. The cauls are made of 18 mm lath, with 25 by 25 mm blocks glued to the ends.

Equally useful on any continuous curve, this type of caul is always made specifically to fit the individual project. Each lath piece is cut 6 mm shorter than half the circumference of the piece being clamped, leaving a 6 mm gap between blocks before clamping. The block length may vary from 18 to 50 mm, depending on the curve: for a shallow curve, use a long block; for a tight curve, a short block.

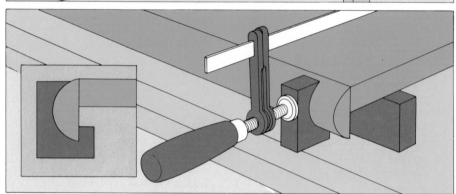

A contoured caul for rounded edging. Curved on one side to conform to the half-round edging that is being glued to a tabletop, this shaped caul provides a flat surface on the other side for the jaw of a cramp. A lip on the caul hooks under the bottom of the edging, to hold it vertically as well as horizontally when the cramp is tightened *(inset)*.

Improvising Devices for Clamping Mitre Joints

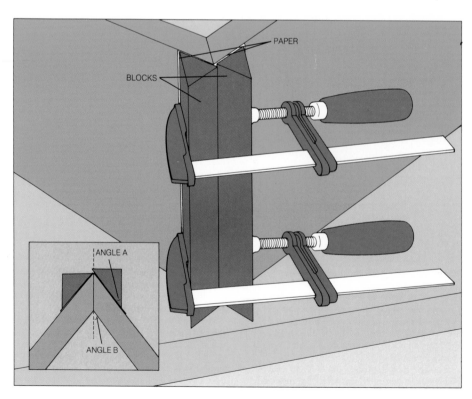

Adding blocks. Pairs of triangular blocks glued over brown paper and then to the sides of deep mitred corners create parallel clamping surfaces. The brown paper allows the blocks to be knocked away once the joint is set; any residue can then be sanded away.

Cut a piece of 25 by 25 mm scrap timber to the same length as the width of the joint, and saw the block diagonally down its length to provide two triangular blocks. Glue brown paper to one side of each block and glue the blocks, without clamping them, to the mitred pieces. Overlap the joint with one of the blocks to provide additional support. Depending on the depth of the joint, use one or two cramps to hold the work firmly as it sets.

If the joint to be assembled is not a right angle, shape the blocks to fit the angle. The angle between the paper-covered side of the block and the side that holds the clamp (angle A) should be equal to angle B—that is, one half the angle of the mitre joint *(inset)*.

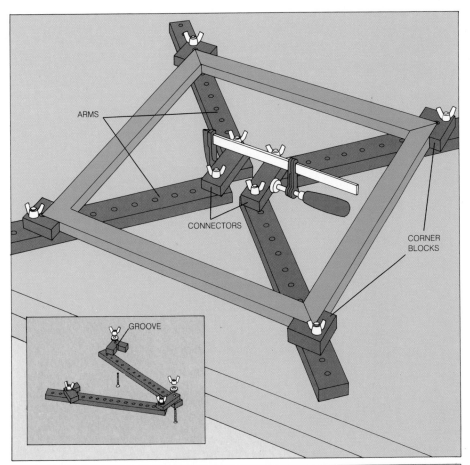

ARMS

CONNECTORS

CORNER
BLOCKS

GROOVE

A wooden jig for mitred frames. Clamped by a single cramp, the two identical halves of this adjustable jig pull together the four mitred corners of a frame. The corner blocks can be positioned at 25 mm intervals along the length of the arms to grip frames of varying size.

To make the jig, cut four hardwood arms that are 18 mm thick, 50 mm wide and as long as needed for the frames you intend to glue. Drill holes down their centre lines every 25 mm to accept 6 mm bolts. Join each pair of arms with hardwood connectors, cut to span the last two holes and held in place with bolts, washers and wing nuts *(inset)*. Cut the four angled corner blocks from hardwood also, and hollow out a shallow groove along their inside corners to provide an escape route for excess glue squeezed from the mitre joint. Drill holes in the blocks to match the holes in the arms, and secure them to the arms with wing nuts, bolts and washers.

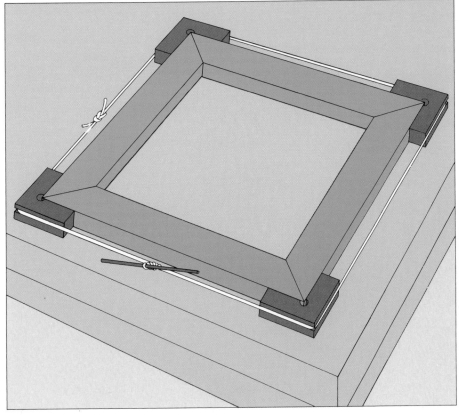

Applying pressure with a tourniquet. A strong cord encircling four corner blocks and twisted by a dowel makes a simple cramp that can solve difficult problems. The blocks that clasp the pieces being joined have horizontal grooves for the cord and shallow vertical grooves along their inside corners to serve as escape routes for excess glue. To tighten the cramp, twist the cord with the dowel, then fix the dowel in place by bracing it between the work and the tabletop. The blocks can be cut to fit any shape—pentagons, hexagons, even asymmetrical joinings that defy the grip of conventional cramps.

3 Shaping by Hand or Machine

In years past, the shaping of wood was done primarily with hand tools, and the pitfalls of inexperience were overcome during long years of apprenticeship. Under the direction of a master craftsman, the aspiring woodworker learnt about wood by holding it in his hands, sensing in his fingers its resistance or pliancy under every stroke of the plane and every probe of the gouge. He learnt that when a spokeshave began to buck or chatter in the middle of a cut, it was fighting against the grain—that it was time to shift his tool and cut in the opposite direction. And he knew that if he tried to carve soft wood into a spindle, his chisel would pull on the soft grain and produce a ragged contour.

Today, power tools do in minutes the tedious shaping jobs that once took hours of work—a boon to home craftsmen, for whom woodworking is likely to be a part-time hobby. A band saw, for instance, can be used to trim away surrounding waste wood, quickly defining an intricate shape even in very thick stock. Used with care and a little imagination, this saw's continuous blade will make fast work of many difficult jobs such as roughing out a cabriole leg or rounding a broad tabletop. Equally effective are the power sanding tools that can grind out complex shapes, either gentle or severe.

But the speed and almost instantaneous facility that power tools provide can be a mixed blessing to the novice. To a degree, power tools may preclude knowledge that can be acquired only through the intimacy of touch. Indeed, some expert woodcraft instructors discourage any use of power tools until the woodworker has mastered hand tools. This approach is rigorous but not without merit. The principal advantage of working with a hand tool is that each stroke of the tool can be adapted to the specific piece of wood. If a surface is knotted, tool pressure is lessened to avoid tearing out the knot. If the wood grain swirls, its pattern can be followed for the smoothest possible cut. Thus, working with hand tools forces the woodworker to learn as much about the material as about the tools.

The truth is that both hand and power tools have a place in shaping wood. Past craftsmen learnt how to minimize their efforts—they knew when to switch from a heavy tool to a more delicate one, and precisely which tool was most appropriate to the job in hand. Modern woodworkers develop the same instincts. They learn to let their power tools bear the brunt of the work, then finish the job with hand tools. If a band saw, jigsaw or power sander will speed up a job, they are put to use. But when the shortcuts are over and the final contours are to be cut, only hand-tool precision will do. At this point, wood shaping is the same demanding craft it has always been. It requires patience, methodical care and a certain reverence for wood.

Cutting Curves in Wood with Power Tools

Curved wood that ultimately appears in graceful furniture and architectural trim begins to take shape, nine times out of ten, on a band saw. This large power tool *(page 19)* saves the modern woodworker hours of time, cutting rough curves which can later be refined with hand tools *(pages 84–89)*. You can cut almost any curved design on a band saw if you know the tricks that enable you to cope with its limitations.

The most rigid of the band saw's limitations is the depth of the "throat"—the distance between the blade and the housing at the back of the machine for the return run of the blade. In home workshop models, the throat of the band saw is only 240 to 360 mm wide, so the width of wood that can pass through is very restricted.

To keep the throat from blocking your progress when you cut large shapes, you may have to stop in the middle of a cut and saw through a waste area to the edge of the board, then begin the cut again in another direction. You can change direction by turning off the saw, backtracking along the cut, and then starting a new cut that will pass through the original one. You can, if nothing else works, draw guidelines on both sides of the wood so that you can turn the board over when necessary. In certain cases—when cutting a circular tabletop as shown on pages 79–81, for example—you can make a jig that allows you to cut a large shape in spite of the restrictions imposed by the throat depth.

Smaller curves present fewer difficulties unless they are so small that the blade cannot follow them without binding. Strategically placed pilot holes and tangential or radial cuts made through waste wood *(pages 78–79)* provide the solutions to many problems of this kind.

Using the right blade for the job will also help you to overcome the tool's limitations. The most commonly used blade is 6 mm wide; it will cut a curve with a radius as small as 15 mm in wood up to 35 mm thick. There are narrower blades for ever tighter curves—a 3 mm blade will cut a curve with a 6 mm radius, but only in wood no thicker than 20 mm. Wider blades will cut thicker wood, but as the width increases the possibility of cutting tight curves decreases. Blades 18 mm and wider will cut shallow curves in timber up to 150 mm thick.

When curves are too tight and the work too fine to be managed on a band saw, use the smaller, less powerful jigsaw, which is available in both portable and bench models. It can be fitted with a variety of delicate blades.

The blade on a jigsaw moves up and down rapidly rather than spinning in a continuous band and, since both ends of the blade can be detached, the saw can cut out curved sections inside a pattern where no waste area leads to the cut. A pilot hole drilled through the pattern provides the starting point, and the blade is inserted through the hole *(page 83)*.

Cutting curves on a band saw or a jigsaw requires great care: note the special safety rules which are given on page 14. It is not practical to use a push stick for guiding wood through a curved cut and this means that your hands will be close to the blade as you guide the wood. Try always to keep your fingers at least 100 mm from the blade while you are working.

Never force the wood forwards when you cut curves—the blade may snap.

Before making any cut, be sure all parts of the tool are properly adjusted. For setting blade guides and adjusting blade tension on a band saw, see page 20. Jigsaw instructions are given on page 83.

Guiding a Band Saw Along a Simple Curve

Cutting a curve. Mark out the curve on the stock, place the wood on the saw table, adjust the blade guide and turn on the saw. Push the board forwards with one hand, guiding it with the other so that the cut is slightly to the waste side of the guideline. Apply steady, constant pressure, pushing as fast as the blade will easily cut. The correct amount of pressure is important: if you push too slowly or stop in the middle of a cut, the spinning blade will burn the wood; if you push too hard, you may break the blade or make an uneven cut.

For a long cut, or if your progress is blocked by the saw's throat, take the blade out of the wood by cutting to the edge of the board through the waste area; then reposition the board, and cut back in from another point.

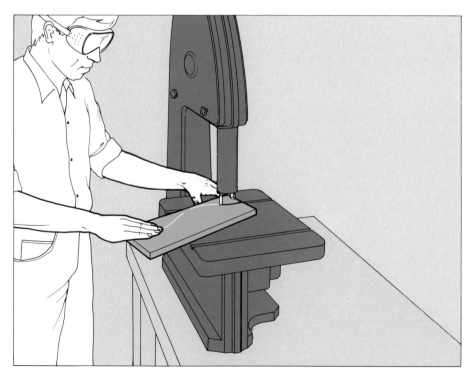

Cutting parallel curves. To draw a curve parallel to one already cut, set the legs of a carpenter's compass to the planned width of the finished piece, then move the compass point along the cut curves so that the pencil point scribes a corresponding second guideline on the wood. Be sure that you are holding the compass perpendicular to the two points of contact. Set the blade guide and cut the second curve.

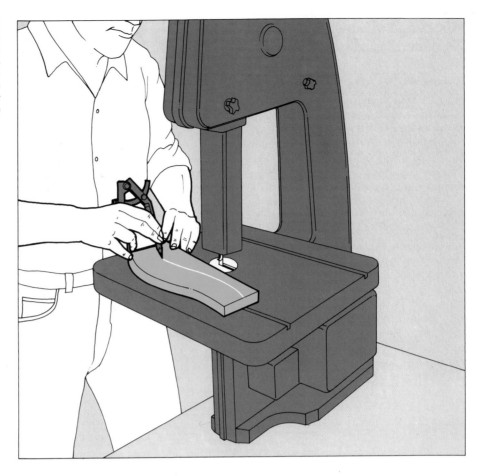

Cutting Stacked Boards for Identical Curves

Cutting several pieces at once. Cut a stack of thin boards in one operation to obtain a set of identical curved shapes. Draw the pattern on one piece of wood or plywood, then stack similar pieces under the pattern piece to form a pile no higher than 150 mm. Drive lost-head nails through the waste corners of the stack so that the points protrude through the piece on which you have drawn the pattern. Put the stack of pieces on the saw table, turn on the saw and cut along the guideline.

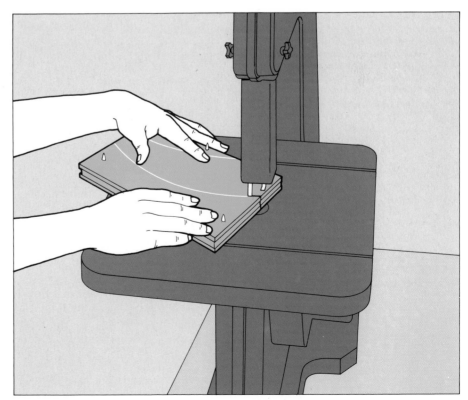

Adapting the Saw to Scrolls and Circles

A turning hole for a tight inside curve. Drill turning holes about 2 mm greater in diameter than the blade width to give you room to manoeuvre the saw blade inside a tight curve. Drill each hole so that a section of its circumference touches the curved guideline you have marked out. To cut round the curve, follow the guideline until you reach the hole, then take the blade through the hole without stopping the saw and continue following the guideline on the other side.

To make a square inside corner, first drill a round pilot hole in the corner, then use a chisel and a mallet *(page 57)* to square off the corner *(inset)*. Run the saw blade along the guideline into the hole; then turn the wood 90 degrees and continue cutting along the guideline.

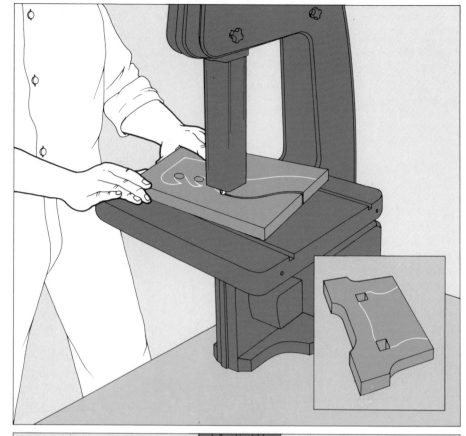

Tangential cuts for a sharp outside curve. Use tangential cuts to manoeuvre round the outside of a sharp curve if the saw blade binds. Start the cut on as straight a section of the guideline as possible, and cut towards the curve. When the blade begins to bind, veer off the guideline and off the edge of the board, cutting away a section of the waste area *(inset)*. Stop the saw, remove the waste section from the saw table, and resume the cut on the guideline, moving the wood along until the blade starts to bind again. Then make another tangential cut. Repeat as necessary to round the curve.

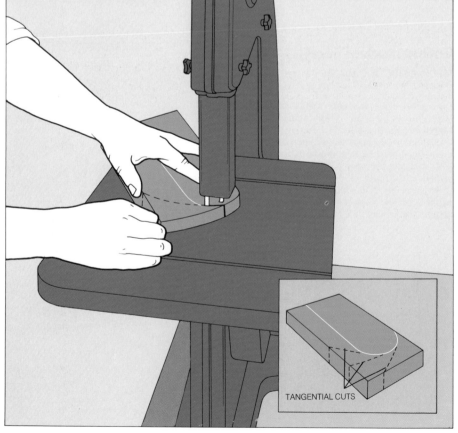

TANGENTIAL CUTS

Radial cuts for a tight, continuous curve. To ease the saw blade round the outside of a tight, continuous curve—in this example a small disc—first make a series of radial cuts from the edges of the board through the waste area towards the guideline. Space the cuts 12 to 25 mm apart, arranged like the spokes of a wheel. Stop each cut slightly short of the guideline. When you come to cut round the outside of the guideline, the pieces of waste wood will fall off.

Setting Up a Jig to Saw a Large Circular Shape

1 Enlarging the saw table. Cut two 100 by 50 mm boards to equal the length of the saw table plus the radius of the planned disc. Tilt the throat end of the saw table up, and fasten the boards to the table's sides with screws driven through the pre-drilled holes in the table edges. Be sure that the top edge of each board is flush with the tabletop and that one end of each is flush with the edge of the table nearest the throat.

From 12 mm plywood, cut a rectangle 50 mm wider than the distance between the outside faces of the 100 by 50 mm boards and 300 mm longer than the radius of the planned disc.

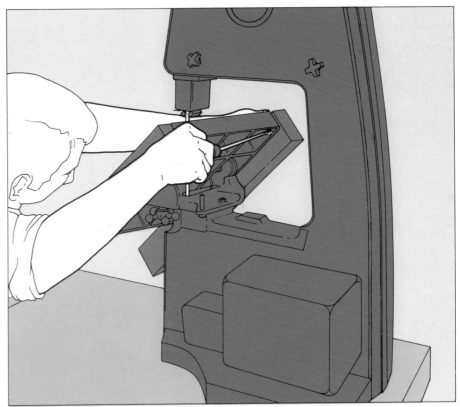

2 **Cutting the jig.** Place the plywood rectangle *(page 79, Step 1)* on the saw table, so that about 150 mm of it is to the left of the blade. Turn on the saw, and cut until the far edge of the board overhangs the far 100 by 50 mm board by 25 mm; stop the saw but leave the board in place.

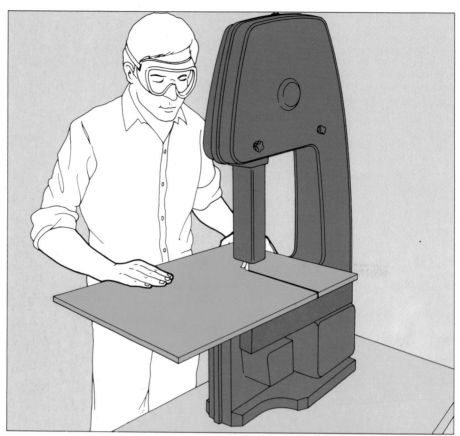

3 **Marking the radius and installing a pivot.** Place a steel square on top of the plywood, with the short arm towards you, the corner just touching the cutting edge of the blade, and the long arm to the right of and perpendicular to the side of the blade. Measuring on the long arm, draw a line out from the blade, equal in length to the radius of the disc you are going to cut. Mark the end of the line, indicating the centre of the disc. Remove the plywood from the table without turning on the saw.

Drill a pilot hole through the plywood at the centre point of the disc and, from the underside of the board, drive a 50 mm screw through the hole until its tip protrudes 6 mm *(Step 4, inset)*. The tip will serve as a pivot while the disc is cut.

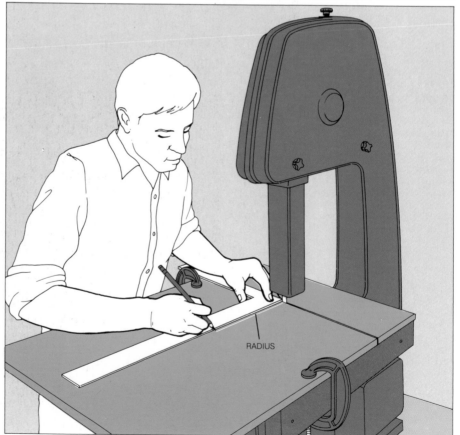

RADIUS

4 **Fastening the jig to the saw table.** Reposition the plywood on the saw table by sliding the kerf past the stationary blade, and clamp the plywood in place. Then drill two pilot holes through the jig edges into each 100 by 50 mm board, countersinking the holes for the screw heads. Fasten the jig to the boards with 37 mm flat-head screws.

5 **Marking the stock for cutting.** Square off the stock from which you plan to cut the large disc *(pages 16–18)*, then draw a guideline for an entrance cut. To do this, first draw two corner-to-corner diagonal lines on the underside of the stock; the point where they intersect will be the centre of the disc. Measuring with a steel square, draw a line the length of the planned radius, extending out from the centre point. From the end of this radius line, draw a perpendicular entrance-cut guideline extending to the edge of the stock. Transfer this line to the top side.

At the centre point on the underside, make a dimple 3 mm deep by tapping a centre punch or a nail punch into the wood with a mallet.

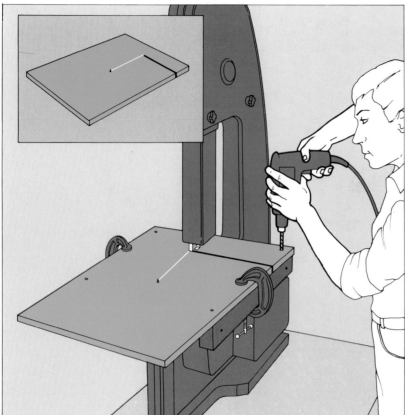

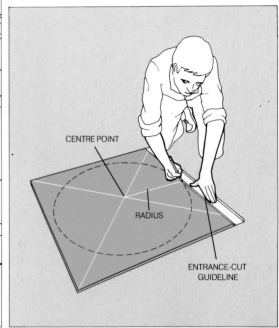

CENTRE POINT

RADIUS

ENTRANCE-CUT GUIDELINE

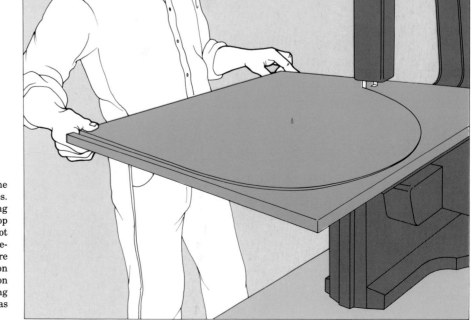

6 **Cutting the disc.** Retract the pivot screw at the centre of the jig so that its tip no longer protrudes. Place the stock right-side up on the jig, cut along the entrance-cut guideline to the end, and stop the saw. Reach under the jig, screw the pivot screw back up to protrude 6 mm and, looking between the jig and the stock, gently manoeuvre the stock until the dimple at the centre rests on the tip of the pivot screw. Then turn the saw on again and feed the stock into the blade, rotating the wood on the pivot screw until the disc has been completely cut.

Outlining the Profile of a Compound Curve

1 **Drawing the guidelines.** Make a paper template of the curved shape to be rough-cut—in this case, a cabriole chair leg—and square off a piece of wood to encompass the widest dimensions of the shape *(pages 16–18)*. Trace the template on one face of the stock, turn the template over, and trace it on an adjoining face so that identical parts meet at the same points along one edge of the stock *(inset)*.

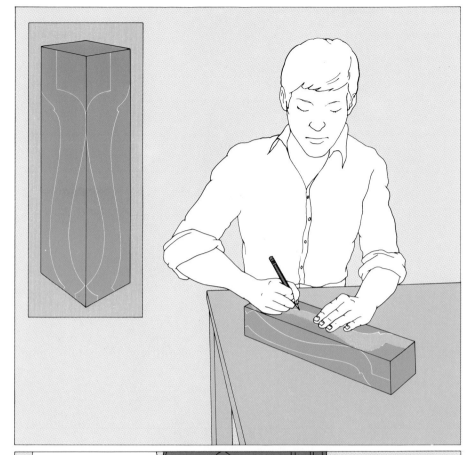

2 **Making the first pair of cuts.** Set the stock on the saw table with one outlined profile facing up; cut along both sides of the profile. Then tack the waste wood back in place temporarily *(inset)*, taking care not to drive a nail into any area that will be part of the finished shape.

3 **Making the second pair of cuts.** Set the stock on the saw table so that the second pair of guidelines is facing up; cut the one on the left first, as shown, then the one on the right. Discard all sections of waste wood.

To smooth and finish the roughed-out shape, use the hand tools and the techniques that are described on pages 84–89.

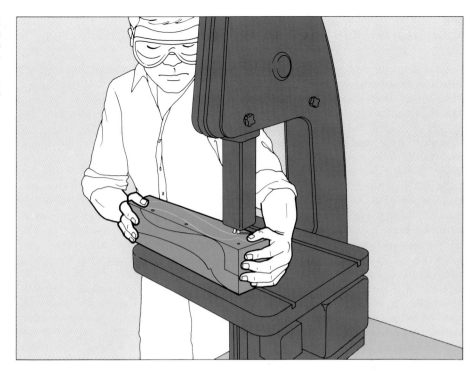

Making an Inside Cut with a Jigsaw

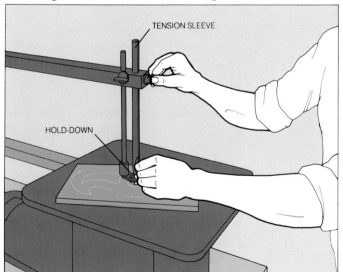

TENSION SLEEVE

HOLD-DOWN

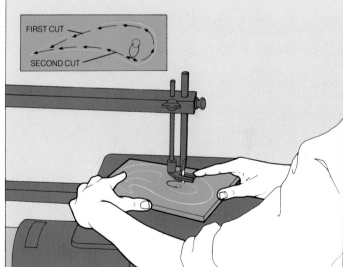

FIRST CUT

SECOND CUT

1 **Setting the blade for the cut.** Drill a pilot hole through the wood within the guidelines for the curved section to be cut out. Disconnect the blade and slip it through the pilot hole from the underside of the workpiece. Slide the workpiece down on to the saw table and replace the blade in the upper chuck. Adjust the hold-down knob so the hold-down is barely touching the top of the wood.

2 **Making the cut.** Turn on the saw, and feed the wood into the blade until you reach the guideline. If all the curves in the cutout are gradual, make the cut in one continuous pass, feeding the wood so that the blade follows the guideline all the way round the cutout to the starting position. Turn off the saw and disconnect the saw blade; remove the work from the saw table.

If, as shown, there is a point in the curve where the blade will be unable to turn, follow the guideline round the gradual curves until the blade can go no further. Stop the saw, and backtrack along the kerf into the pilot hole; then cut along the guideline in a different direction, to the point where you stopped before *(inset)*.

Contouring Wood with Hand Tools

Wood grain, with its flowing lines and interesting irregularities, has attracted the imagination of craftsmen since time began, lending itself to a seemingly endless variety of shapes. Today the preliminary steps in crafting wood are often performed with power tools such as the band saw *(page 76)*. But hand tools, as always, are indispensable for the finishing touches that give shaped wood its special beauty. The tools on these pages have been used for centuries, many of them remaining essentially unchanged in design.

Every hand tool is designed for a specific purpose, and to use it properly requires the mastery of a particular technique. The drawknife, for example, is used to debark logs and bring timber to rough shape by removing waste wood; as its name suggests, it is pulled towards the worker, and it demands both strength and considerable skill to use accurately and effectively. Spokeshaves, which are used to smooth curved edges, are generally pushed, and require a much more delicate handling technique.

Planes, which are pushed, come in an astonishing array of shapes and sizes. The diminutive thumb plane fits easily into areas where planes with wider blades cannot go; the compass plane, with its flexible steel sole plate, moulds itself to the contours of broad curved surfaces, both convex and concave. The forming tool, its cutting face covered with tiny blades with holes between them for the shavings to pass through, rounds off square corners.

The greatest disadvantage of the cutting tools is that they have a tendency to lift and break exposed grain ends as they cut. These tools cut most successfully when following the direction of the wood grain, which makes them particularly difficult to use in tight spots and on woods with irregular grains, such as bird's-eye maple.

Rasps, files and rifflers have tiny teeth that tear wood rather than cut it—this makes them convenient to use in any direction, regardless of grain. They are excellent tools for smoothing shaped surfaces and are invaluable in the finishing of intricately carved wood. However, they too have one disadvantage. In tearing the wood fibres, these tools—especially the coarser surfaced—leave numerous tiny scratches that can obscure the grain pattern and dull the surface. This effect can be diminished by using a finer-toothed tool.

For the final smoothing of all wood, rub down the surface with progressively finer grit sizes of sandpaper. Start with grit size 60 and finish with size 180 or even—for an exceptionally smooth surface—size 240.

Caring for cutting and scraping tools is simple but necessary. The blades of drawknives, planes and spokeshaves must be kept razor sharp; hone them on an oilstone. The teeth of rasps and files should be cleaned with a file-card—a type of brush with soft wire bristles.

Rough Shaping with a Drawknife

Making a concave cut with a drawknife. After outlining the cut on the wood, clamp the timber in a vice, angling it slightly towards you. Lay the drawknife blade across the far end of the proposed cut, the bevel of the cutting edge facing down. Tilt the blade slightly down and pull it towards you, making a shallow cut to the lowest point of the outline. As you pull, lift the tool handles to prise away wood chips. Repeat this initial cut, following the path of the outline and cutting more deeply into the wood each time. Keep cutting towards the low point until the resulting wood chips no longer break off easily. Then reverse the wood in the vice.

Cut the other side in the same way, working from the end towards the low point *(inset)*. As you near the low point, make shallow, slicing cuts, removing the wood in thin shavings to avoid breaking the grain on the first side of the cut.

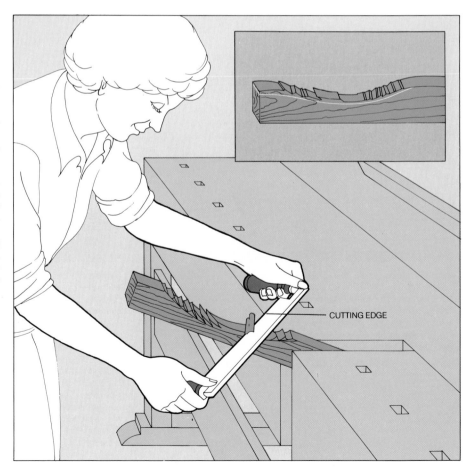

CUTTING EDGE

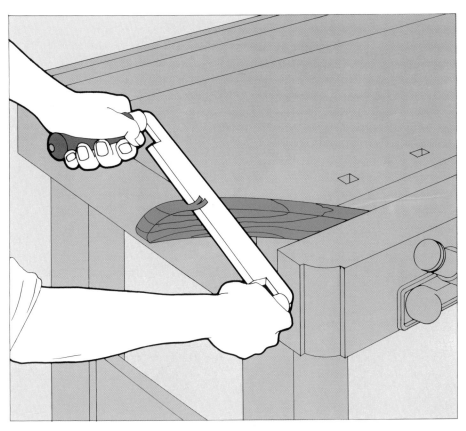

Making a convex cut with a drawknife. For a convex cut, begin at the high point of the curve and cut down and away from it; when both gradual and sharp curves are included in the design, as on the chair-back stile shown here, cut the sharper curve first. Hold the drawknife blade across the wood, bevel up and at approximately a 30-degree angle to the wood. Pull the blade towards you with shallow, shearing cuts that produce thin shavings. Continue cutting in this way until the curve is the desired shape.

For the more gradual section of the curve, set the blade perpendicular to the wood and, again beginning at the high point of the curve, pull the knife towards you with shallow strokes until you have formed an even, continuous curve that meets the cut section. Then reverse the wood in the vice and cut the opposite end, starting as before at the high point of the curve.

Rounding a Corner with a Forming Tool

Curving a right-angled joint. Clamp the joint in a vice, pointed corner facing up. Hold the forming tool in both hands—one hand grasping the rear handle to push the tool, the other hand resting on the front of the tool to guide it. To round one side of the joint, hold the cutting face at an angle of about 5 degrees to the wood surface facing you. Set the tool on the joint and, applying gentle steady pressure, push the cutting face half way over the corner, ending the movement with the tool in a horizontal position. Make as many cuts as necessary to round half of the corner, then reverse the joint in the vice and repeat the cuts to shape the other side.

On a joint such as the finger joint shown here, where the grain direction changes abruptly, work slowly. The forming tool's teeth are arranged for a diagonal slicing cut *(inset)*, designed to deal with varying grain directions, but any sudden changes require deft and careful control.

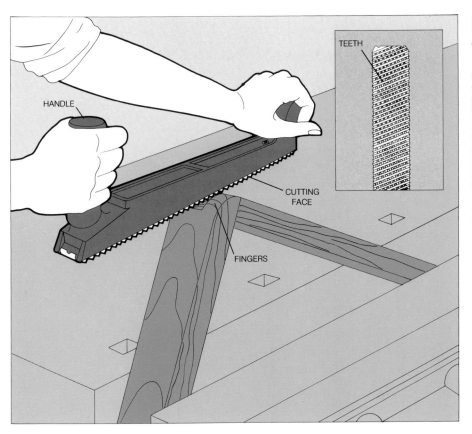

HANDLE

TEETH

CUTTING FACE

FINGERS

Versatile Spokeshaves for Smoothing Curves

Planing a curved edge. After shaping the face of a curve with a band saw *(page 76)*, smooth down its edges with a spokeshave. A round-faced spokeshave, whose rounded sole allows maximum contact with the wood surface on concave curves, can be used to smooth either convex or concave curves; a flat-faced spokeshave should be used for convex curves only.

Grasp the spokeshave handles by resting your thumbs in the indented thumb rests on top of the handles and your index fingers on either side of the front, or nose, of the tool. With gentle pressure and repeated strokes, push the spokeshave along the edge of the curve, lifting thin shavings. Wherever possible, you should work in the direction of the grain—planing against the grain may tear the wood fibres.

To adjust the spokeshave blade, loosen the thumbscrew on the covering cap, and turn the adjustment screws until the blade barely protrudes beyond the opening in the sole plate *(inset)*. Then tighten the thumbscrew.

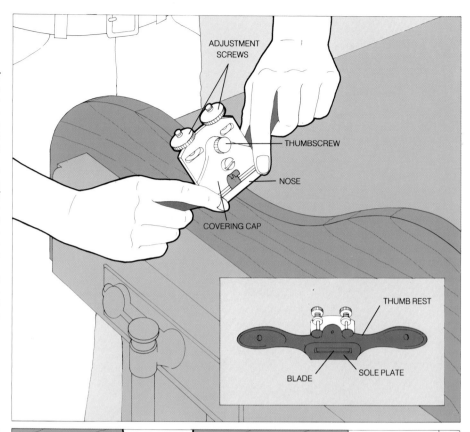

Smoothing a rounded edge. Using a half-round spokeshave with a curved blade, grasp the handles by pressing your thumbs against the rear faces and wrapping your fingers around the front. Tilt the back of the spokeshave slightly towards you, set the blade on the corner of the edge and push the tool away from you with gentle, steady strokes. If the grain direction changes, reverse the tool, tilt the top away from you and pull the spokeshave towards you with the same stroking motion.

To adjust the half-round spokeshave to make as shallow a cut as possible, simply loosen the thumbscrew—which releases the blade and the covering cap—and move the blade into the required position by hand.

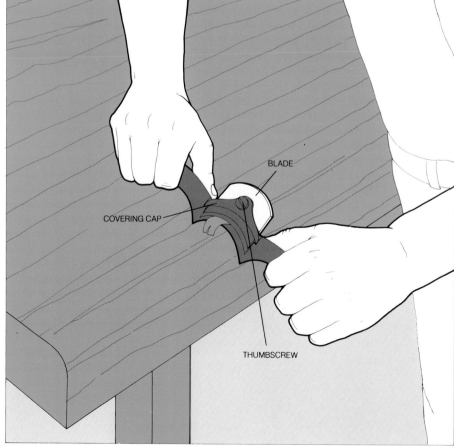

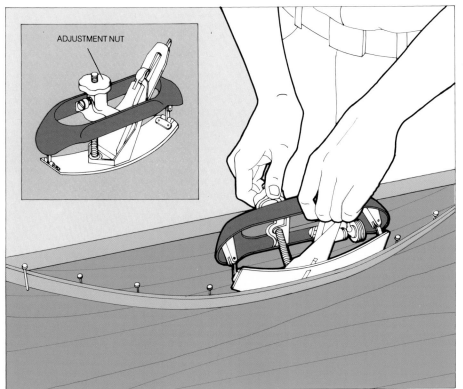

A Flexible Plane That Follows Curved Surfaces

1 **Adjusting the flexible sole plate.** First establish the proposed curve by cutting a strip of 18 mm lath to the desired length of the curve and setting it on edge between two nails driven into the face of the wood where the curve will begin and end. Wedge the lath between the nails, allowing it to form a smooth curve, then anchor it with supporting nails driven against the waste side of the curve at 100 mm intervals.

Use the curved lath as a guide for adjusting the sole plate of a compass plane. For a concave curve, as here, lay the plane on its side against the inside curve of the lath; turn the adjusting nut until the sole-plate curve is slightly sharper than the lath curve. For a convex curve, lay the plane on its side against the outside curve of the lath and adjust the sole plate to a curve slightly flatter than that of the lath. Then trace the outline of the lath on the wood, remove the lath and, using a band saw, rough-cut the curve to within 3 mm of the outline.

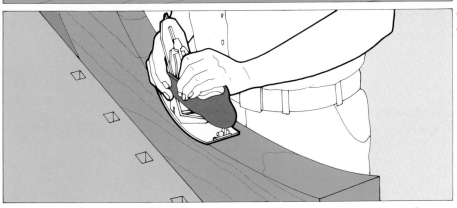

2 **Smoothing the rough-cut curve.** Set the rough-cut wood in a vice. Grasp the back of the compass plane with one hand, guide the front with the other, and push the plane along the wood, following the pencilled outline with long, smooth strokes. Work parallel with the direction of the grain, never across it or at an angle to it. For a concave cut, as here, start at the ends of the curve and move towards its low point; as you approach the low point, shorten your strokes to avoid tearing the exposed grain ends. For a convex curve, start at the high point of the curve and work down towards the ends.

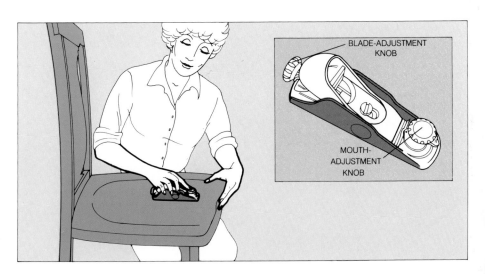

A Small Plane for Tight Places

Using a block plane. Hold the block plane between your thumb and your index and middle fingers, with the index finger on the mouth adjustment knob at the nose. Push down and forward with short, light strokes, guiding the tool with the index finger so that you are always working parallel with the grain.

Most of the smoothing done with a block plane requires a shallow cut. To adjust the blade, turn the knob at the back of the plane until the blade barely protrudes beyond the opening in the sole plate (*inset*).

Tools That Shape Wood
by Scraping It

A battery of rasps, files and rifflers. Rasps and files have toothed scraping surfaces that are 150 to 300 mm long, with a tang at one end that fits snugly into a wooden handle. The scraping surface may take one of three forms; flat on both sides (as in these examples), round on one face and flat on the other, or completely round. The difference between them is that rasps, which have tiny individual teeth arranged in staggered rows, are generally used for rougher work; files, whose teeth are formed by long grooves cut at an angle across the tool face, are used for a smoother, finer finish.

Both rasps and files come in varying degrees of coarseness, which is determined by the number of teeth per unit of scraping surface. The bastard-cut rasp shown here *(below, left)* is used for rough shaping of hardwoods; for rough shaping of softwoods, a medium-cut rasp is used. A smooth-cut rasp has over twice as many teeth per unit of scraping surface as the bastard-cut rasp, in an apparently random pattern; it produces more finished results. The single-cut file, with grooves running in only one direction, and the more abrasive double-cut file, with crisscrossing grooves, are available in the same variety of coarseness designations as rasps.

Rifflers *(below, right)* are double-ended tools with spatulate, curved or pointed heads; they are useful for cleaning intricately carved details and for shaping hard-to-reach spots. Their scraping surfaces are miniature versions of rasps and files, and they come in the same range of coarseness.

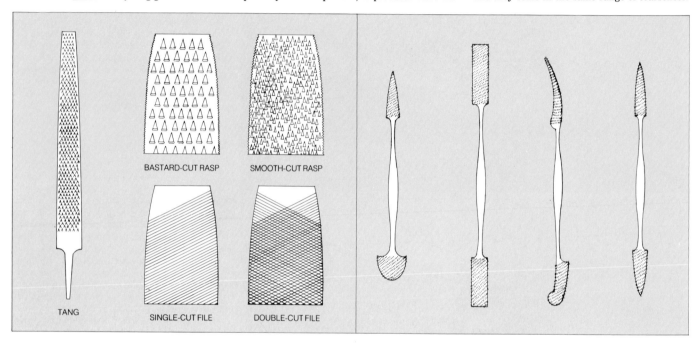

BASTARD-CUT RASP   SMOOTH-CUT RASP

TANG

SINGLE-CUT FILE   DOUBLE-CUT FILE

Techniques for Using
Scraping Tools

Working with a rasp or a file. Rasps and files are held in the same way—diagonally, with one hand on the handle to push the tool and the heel of the other hand resting on the front of the tool to guide it. Use a gentle forward stroke to scrape the wood; then lift the tool and move it backwards to repeat the stroke, to avoid dulling the teeth. Depending on the results desired, rasps and files can be pushed in any direction along or across the grain. To finish and smooth a concave cut, as in this example, push the curved face of a half-round rasp down towards the low point of the curve, working diagonally across the grain with a gentle, upward stroke. For a convex shape, start at the high point of the curve and work down, using the flat side of the same tool and an up-and-over rocking motion diagonally across the grain of the wood.

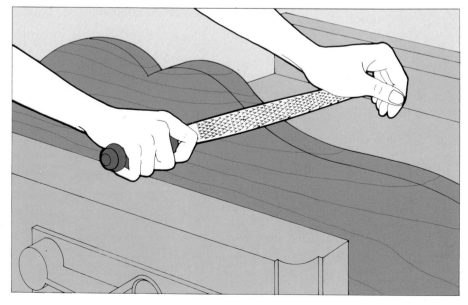

Getting into tight confines with a riffler. Pick a riffler to fit the cut—in this example, a curved riffler is used to smooth a narrow, routed channel outlining the edge of a table apron. Hold the riffler in one hand, using the index finger of that hand and the thumb of the other hand to guide the tool as you push it. Never pull the riffler back along its path; lift it up from the work and reposition it to repeat the smoothing cut.

A Chair Shaped Completely with Hand Tools

From the top of its curving backrest to the bottoms of its mock-claw feet, the contours of the chair shown here were smoothed and refined with hand-held shaping tools. The concave and convex profile of the backrest *(inset, top)* was cut first on a band saw *(page 76)*; then the gentle curves were shaped with a spokeshave and the sharper curves with a file. The broad shallow curves of the front and back faces of the backrest were shaped with the flexible sole plate of a compass plane. A jigsaw was used to rough-cut the harp-shaped splat *(page 83)*; the edges were smoothed with a spokeshave and a riffler, the latter taking care of the tight spots.

On the gently contoured seat of the chair *(inset, centre)*, a forming tool established the shape; a block plane was then used to refine it. The curved edges of the seat were smoothed with a smooth-cut rasp. The long curves of the stiles and legs were rough-cut first on a band saw, and were then smoothed with a spokeshave. The smaller, deeply incised curves of the mock-claw feet *(inset, bottom)* were carved out first with a band saw and then smoothed with rifflers.

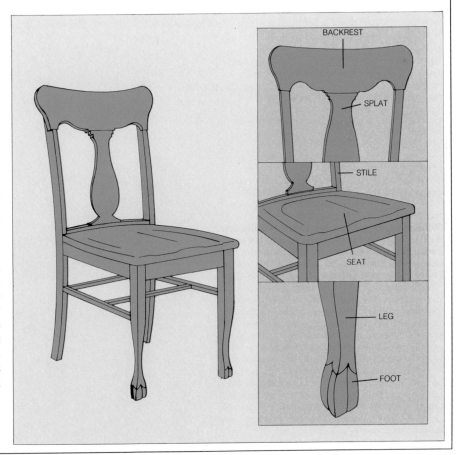

Wood-Turning with a Lathe

Although the electric motor has replaced the foot treadle as the power that drives a woodworking lathe, the principle remains unchanged: a combination of whirling wood and hand-held carving tools. The idea of turning wood to shape it, known to artisans of the earliest civilizations, has never outlived its usefulness or lost its appeal to craftsmen. The lathe is invaluable to the home carpenter for creating certain kinds of elaborate symmetrical shapes—stair balusters, drawer pulls, newel-post caps and other architectural trim, not to mention furniture legs and wooden bowls.

To a wood-turner, strength is not nearly so important as finesse. Developing a relaxed stance and a proper tool grip are the first steps to accomplish in using a lathe. Once these are mastered and you begin to feel the interplay between the spinning wood and the cutting edges of the tools, learning the various techniques of turning becomes easier.

The special tools designed to shape wood mounted on a lathe fall into two rough categories: cutting tools, which are used to shave away waste wood layer by layer, and scraping tools, which are pushed straight into the wood as it spins and scrape away small particles. With practice, you will develop a feel for holding the cutting and scraping tools at the correct angle.

Selecting the right wood for turning is as important as developing proper techniques. Hardwoods generally are better than softwoods, and close-grained hardwoods such as elm, beech, teak, ash and cherry all produce smooth, crisp-looking results. An open-grained hardwood such as oak is less satisfactory, since it tends to splinter. A softwood such as pine is difficult to turn in intricate shapes, but it is inexpensive and useful for practice. Whatever wood you choose, be sure that it is free of splits and knots. Tool edges catch on such imperfections, and the resulting chips and breaks can ruin a piece of work.

The size of the piece of wood you can turn is determined by the size of your lathe. A typical home workshop lathe will hold a spindle—a narrow piece of wood supported at both ends of the lathe—up to 800 mm long, or a block of wood that has a diagonal measurement of up to 250 mm. Some manufacturers offer a lathe attachment designed for use with a portable electric drill, but on these both power and choice of turning speed are limited by the capacity of the drill motor.

For safety, a lathe must be very stable. A freestanding model should be bolted to the floor, and a benchtop model secured to a heavy bench, which again should be bolted to the floor.

Keeping a lathe in good working order requires only a little time and effort. Oil the moving parts according to the manufacturer's instructions, and always be sure to keep the lathe free of any waste wood that could clog the machinery.

Wood-turning hand tools require more care. Keep cutting edges sharp by honing them on a fine oilstone. Set the bevel of the tool flat on the stone and, with gentle pressure, push the blade around in a figure-of-eight pattern. For a curved bevel such as on a gouge (*opposite page, centre, below*), rock the bevel from side to side as you push it through the figure-of-eight. A few strokes with a slipstone will finish off the inside of a gouge's curved cutting edge.

The anatomy of a wood lathe. Wood that is spun on a lathe is supported between two end parts called the headstock and the tailstock. The headstock is permanently mounted at the motor end of the bed, or base; the tailstock slides along the bed to accommodate wood of various lengths.

The headstock spindle, driven by an electric motor, turns the workpiece. It holds a part called the centre which has spurs or screws that penetrate the wood. Pulleys on the motor and on the lathe, connected by a belt, provide several speeds. The large exposed wheel on the headstock makes it possible to turn the work by hand. The spindle of the tailstock holds the cup centre; it does not rotate the wood and can be moved in and out with a second handwheel, to ensure that the wood is tightly mounted on the lathe.

Between the headstock and the tailstock is a tool rest; it can be moved along the bed and adjusted to various heights and angles. It supports the various cutting and scraping tools (*opposite page*) that are used to shape the wood. For working from end to end of an extended workpiece, a long tool rest can be substituted (*page 94*)

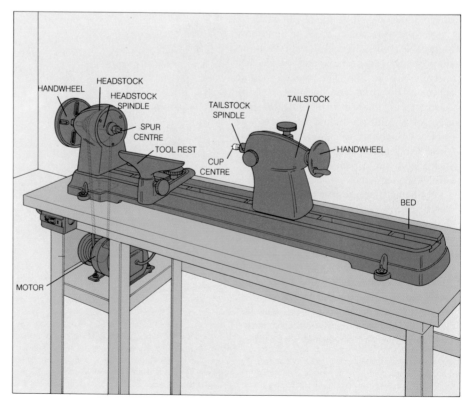

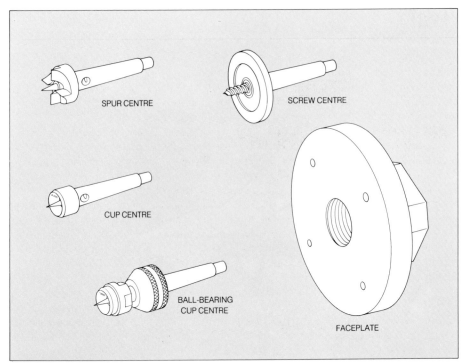

Locking the wood in a lathe. Shown here are five basic spindle centres for holding wood in a lathe. The spur centre, which spins the wood as well as holding it, has four sharp spurs that are embedded in the headstock end of the wood. The cup centre remains stationary in the tailstock spindle; it has a concave end, so only the thin rim and the point penetrate the spinning wood. An alternative centre for use with the tailstock spindle is a cup centre with ball-bearings that permit it to spin freely as the wood turns, reducing friction.

In some lathe work, such as that involved in shaping a wooden bowl, the wood is attached only to the headstock. Work of this kind is done with the faceplate—a metal disc that screws on to the headstock spindle; the wood is fixed to the faceplate with screws. Faceplates range from 75 to 250 mm in diameter, the size chosen depending on the size of the wood block being shaped. The screw centre is used for smaller faceplate turnings, such as drawer pulls.

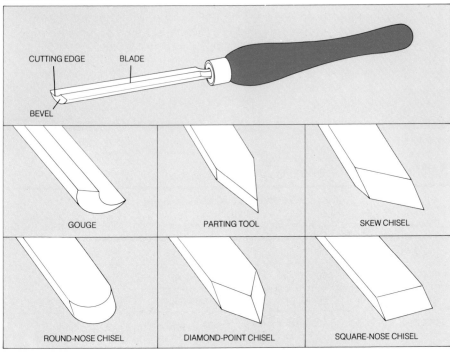

Lathe tools for cutting and scraping. The gouge, the parting tool and the skew chisel are all cutting tools. The gouge has a curved blade with a rounded cutting edge bevelled on the convex side. Gouges range in width from 6 to 25 mm or even more. They are used for reducing rectangular stock to a cylindrical shape and for cutting grooves and coves. The parting tool has two flat sides; its two bevels are angled towards each other to form a narrow cutting edge at the end of the blade. When it is held so that the bevels are vertical, the parting tool is used for making narrow grooves of any desired depth. A skew chisel has a cutting edge that is ground at an angle to the side of the blade. This kind of chisel is used for cutting beads, V-grooves and tapers.

Round-nose, diamond-point and square-nose chisels are scraping rather than cutting tools. They have flat blades of various shapes and are bevelled on one side. Although scraping tools are not positioned in the same way as cutting tools, they can be used to create some of the same shapes. They are also used extensively for faceplate turning *(page 82)*.

(page 82)

Safety Rules for Lathe Use

In addition to applying the safety rules listed for all power tools *(page 14),* take the following precautions when you operate a lathe:

☐ Before starting the lathe, be sure that the wood is well anchored at both ends and that all surfaces will clear the tool rest as the wood spins.

☐ As you turn and shape the wood, stop the lathe periodically and readjust the tool rest to keep it about 6 mm from the wood you are working.

☐ Use a speed chart *(overleaf)* to determine a safe turning speed for each project; never operate the lathe faster than the speed recommended. If you have difficulty controlling the hand tool you are using, reduce the speed.

☐ Be especially careful to avoid the possibility of clothing or hair catching in the moving parts. Do not wear loose clothes, cuffs or ties. Long hair should always be well tied back.

Hand Positions for Holding Lathe Tools

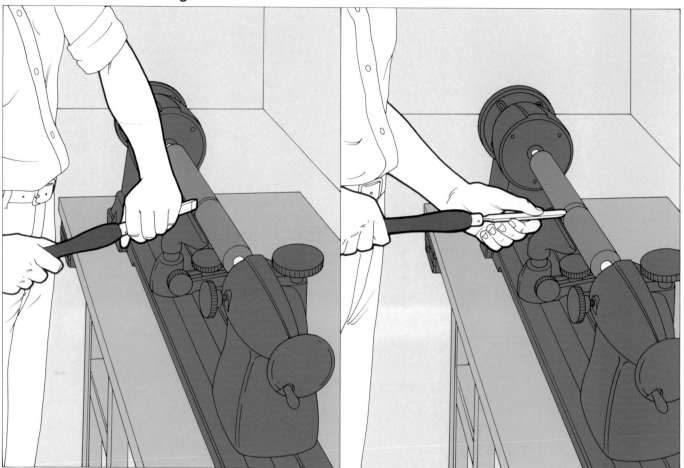

Holding the tool as the wood turns. Grip the end of the tool handle firmly but not tightly with one hand, keeping your forearm close to your body. This arm directs the action of the tool. Hold the tool's blade lightly against the tool rest with the other hand. This hand may be positioned with four fingers on top of the blade and the thumb below it, with the little finger touching the tool rest *(above, left)*. Or you may prefer to put the thumb on top and four fingers below, with the index finger against the tool rest *(above, right)*.

The angle at which a cutting tool is held varies with the hardness of the wood. The softer the wood, the more acute the angle; for hardwoods the tool is laid almost at right angles to the workpiece. With a cutting tool, such as a skew chisel *(above, left)*, hold the bevel against the stock and the blade, angled for the desired cut, against the top of the tool rest. As the wood spins, raise the handle gradually in the direction of the cut, driving the cutting edge into the wood. Here, the skew chisel is being used to cut a V-groove.

With a scraping tool, such as the round-nose chisel *(above, right)*, hold the blade horizontal across the tool rest, the bevel down, and feed the cutting edge straight into the wood. Here, the round-nose chisel is being used to cut a groove.

Setting Turning Speeds to Suit the Job

Diameter of work (mm)	LATHE SPEEDS (revolutions per minute)		
	Roughing cut	Shaping cut	Finishing cut and sanding
less than 50	900–1,400	2,200–2,800	3,000–4,200
50–100	600–1,000	1,800–2,400	2,400–3,400
100–150	600–1,000	1,200–1,800	1,800–2,400
150–200	400–800	800–1,200	1,200–1,800
200–250	300–700	700–1,000	1,000–1,200
more than 250	300–600	600–900	600–900

Choosing the best speed. Recommended lathe-turning speeds are listed in this table, expressed in revolutions per minute. First match the diameter of the stock you are using with the dimensions in the left-hand column of the table; in general, the greater the diameter of the stock, the slower it must be turned. Then at the top of the table find the type of work you want to do. Slow speeds are best for faceplate turning and for shaping rectangular stock into a cylinder. Medium speeds are used for cutting various shapes once you have a cylinder. The fastest speeds are used for final smoothing and sanding. Stock which is unusually narrow or long may vibrate at the recommended speed; if this happens, try the next lower speed. If the lathe is not designed to run at exactly the recommended speed, use the closest lower speed.

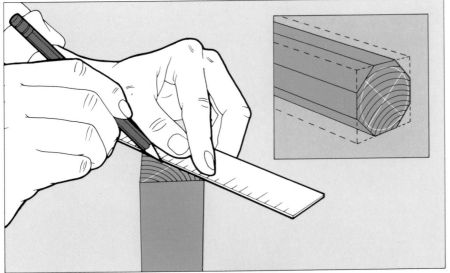

Mounting the Wood in the Machine

1 Finding the centres. After you cut the stock to the desired length on a table saw and carefully square the sides, draw diagonal lines from corner to corner on both ends to locate their centres precisely. If the wood is hard, drill a small hole at the centres; otherwise mark the centres with a centre punch. At the headstock end, use a handsaw to cut a kerf 3 mm deep along each diagonal line.

If the stock is more than 50 mm square, use a compass to scribe the largest possible circle on one end of the stock. Then set a table-saw blade at a 45-degree angle, and bevel the edges of the stock, starting each of the four cuts just outside the scribed circle *(inset)*.

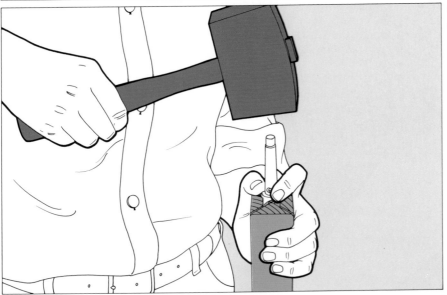

2 Embedding the spur centre. With the spur centre removed from the headstock spindle, set its point at the intersection of the diagonal saw kerfs, with the spurs positioned over the kerfs. Use a wooden mallet to tap the shank of the spur centre lightly, until the spurs are firmly embedded in the wood.

Push the cup-centre shank on to the tailstock spindle and lubricate its centre point with soap or wax. Turn the tailstock handwheel to retract the spindle as far as possible into the tailstock.

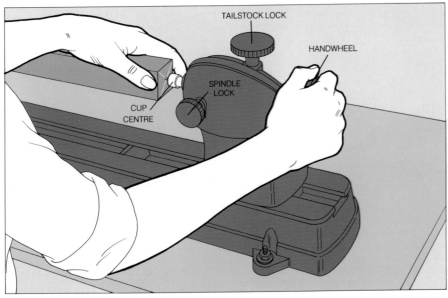

3 Fastening the wood in the lathe. Loosen the tailstock lock so that you can slide the tailstock assembly along the bed away from the headstock. Push the spur-centre shank into the headstock spindle and, as you support the wood with one hand, push the tailstock towards the wood until the point of the cup centre nearly touches the wood. Fasten the tailstock in this position with the tailstock lock.

Turn the tailstock handwheel to drive the cup-centre point into the wood at the intersection of the diagonal pencil lines, until the rim of the cup centre penetrates the wood. Finally, use the tailstock-spindle lock to fix the cup centre in this position. Give the stock a spin by hand; if it wobbles or does not turn freely, you will need to readjust the tailstock spindle.

From Square Stock to Perfectly Round Cylinder

1 **Rough cutting with a lathe gouge.** Secure a long tool rest on the lathe bed and set the tool rest level with the midpoint of the wood being turned, about 3 mm away from it. Turn on the lathe and place a large gouge on the tool rest, 50 mm in from one end of the wood, keeping the handle angled slightly downwards and the concave face of the gouge blade turned towards the opposite end. Push the gouge forward until the bevel touches the wood; then, holding the gouge firmly, raise the tool handle slightly until the cutting edge shears the wood. Draw the gouge along the length of the tool rest, turning its handle gradually so that all parts of the cutting edge come into contact with wood, until it passes off the end of the spinning wood.

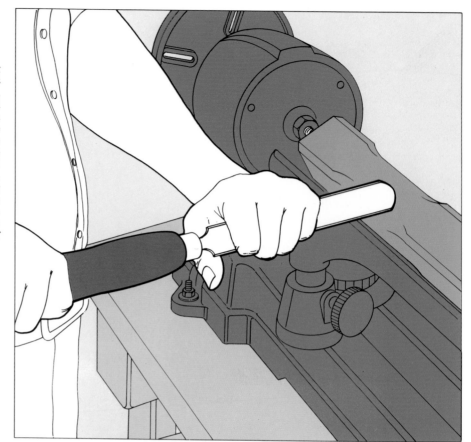

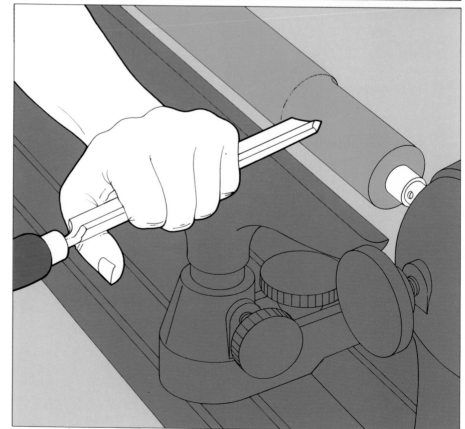

2 **Finishing the rough cut.** Adjust the angle at which you are holding the gouge and draw it back along the tool rest to the starting end, again turning the handle to engage the spinning wood with all parts of the cutting edge. Continue in this manner, drawing the gouge from one end of the tool rest to the other with a gentle rolling motion, until the diameter of the cylinder is about 3 mm greater than the required measurement.

Stop the lathe to move the tool rest closer to the spinning wood and adjust the tailstock when necessary; check the diameter of the cylinder with calipers. Until the wood becomes cylindrical, it will tend to splinter; if splintering is excessive, reduce the lathe speed and make shallower cuts.

3 **Final smoothing with a skew chisel.** Set the tool rest 3 mm from the wood, turn on the lathe, and place a skew chisel on the tool rest 50 mm in from one end of the wood. Angle the handle downwards and hold the blade at a 25 to 30-degree angle to the cylinder. Push forwards so that the bevel touches the wood, but keep the skew point clear of the wood to avoid gashes. Hold the blade lightly against the cylinder; slide it towards the opposite end, directing the lower half of the cutting edge so that you feel very little resistance and the cut produces very thin shavings. Push the blade off the end of the stock.

Reverse the blade position and cut in the same manner along the entire length of the cylinder back to the starting end. Adjust the tool rest when necessary. Repeat the cuts until the cylinder is perfectly smooth.

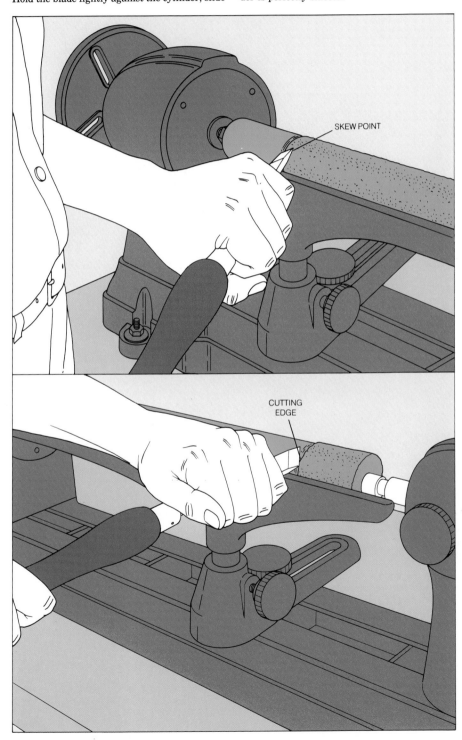

A Shapely Leg That Sums Up the Repertoire of a Lathe

Four basic shapes cut with a lathe. One unusual furniture leg displays the four commonest shapes that can be produced on a lathe. These shapes can be cut in any number and in any order to produce a variety of patterns. A bead is a rounded shape cut with a skew chisel. A taper is wider at one end than at the other and usually is an elongated shape; it is cut with a parting tool, a gouge and a skew chisel. Rectangular sections can be left uncut, except for shoulders, which are rounded with a skew chisel. A cove is a concave section, with equal diameters at the ends and a smaller diameter in the middle; this shape is cut with a parting tool and a gouge.

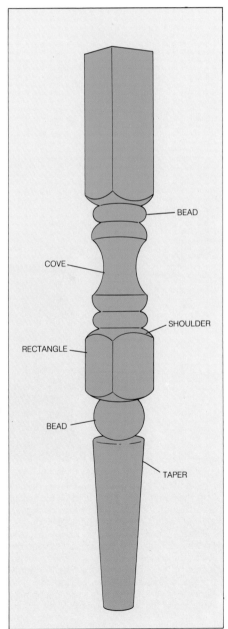

Raising a Bead

1 Making end grooves with a skew chisel. Set the tool rest slightly above the centre of the cylindrical stock and about 6 mm away from it. Switch on the lathe, and mark the sides of the bead by holding a pencil lightly in two places against the spinning cylinder. If the bead is to be wider than 12 mm, add a third guideline midway between the first two lines drawn.

Place a skew chisel on the tool rest, with the blade on edge and the skew point down. Tilt the tool handle very slightly downwards, to make certain the cut will be made just above the midpoint of the stock. Push the skew point straight into the stock at one of the side guidelines, scraping a V-shaped groove 3 mm deep. Cut a groove at the other side guideline in the same way, but do not cut into the centre guideline.

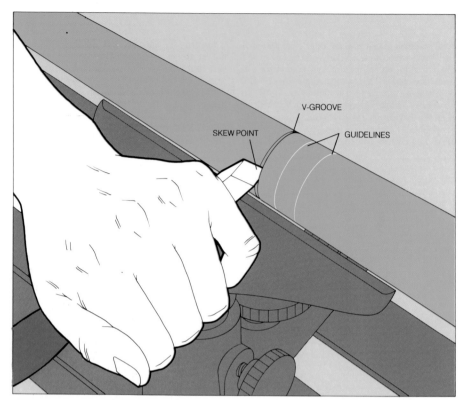

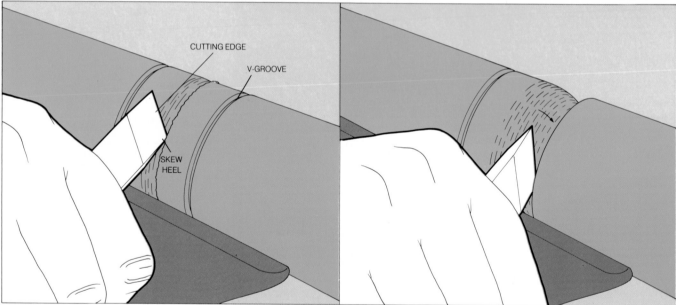

2 Shaping the bead. With the stock spinning, place the blade of the skew chisel almost flat on the tool rest at the centre of the bead. Position the heel of the cutting edge to the right of and lower than the point, with the tool handle angled slightly downwards. Push the blade forwards until the skew's bevel, but not its cutting edge, touches the wood at the centre guideline *(above, left)*. To begin the cut, raise and twist the handle slightly until the bottom half of the cutting edge just shears the wood. Then, in one continuous motion, roll the heel of the blade towards the right groove, raising the handle and pushing the blade forwards into the wood as the chisel turns. End with the skew's cutting edge vertical in the groove, the heel down *(above, right)*. To make the groove deeper for a rounder bead, push the heel of the cutting edge further into the groove before withdrawing the blade.

Cut the other side of the bead, starting with the heel of the cutting edge pointing to the left. Alternate right and left cuts, always cutting "downhill" (from the centre of the bead towards the outside), until the bead is the desired shape.

Incising a Cove

1 **Cutting the V-grooves.** Set the tool rest level with the centre of the stock and 6 mm away from it; turn on the lathe, and mark the sides and centre of the cove on the spinning stock with a pencil. Then place a skew chisel almost on its edge on the tool rest, point up, in line with a side guideline. Hold the blade so that you angle the heel of the cutting edge slightly towards the centre of the planned cove. Keeping the tool handle angled slightly downwards, push the skew's heel into the wood to form an angled V-groove 3 mm deep. For a similar V-groove at the other side of the cove, angle the blade in the opposite direction so that the heel again points towards the centre of the cove; make the second cut *(inset)*.

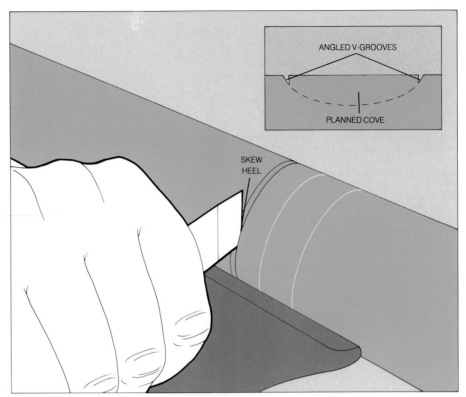

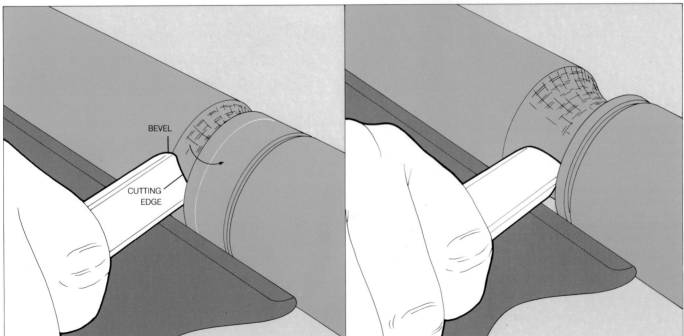

2 **Shaping the cove with a gouge.** Position a gouge almost on its edge on top of the tool rest, holding it so that its bevel rests against a V-groove and its concave side faces towards the centre of the cove. Angle the cutting edge slightly towards the cove centre, the tool handle slightly down and away from it *(above, left)*. Push the cutting edge into the stock and, in one continuous motion, raise the tool handle slightly to push the cutting edge into the wood while rolling the bevel down and to-wards the centre of the cove *(above, right)*. End the cut with the blade horizontal, the bevel down, at the centre of the cove. Be sure that you do not cut past the centre.

Cut the other side of the cove in the same way, but start with the bevel, cutting edge and tool handle angled in the opposite direction. Continue to make cuts in alternating directions, cutting from the outside edges of the cove towards the centre, until the cove is the desired shape.

Creating a Taper

1 **Sizing the taper ends.** Smooth the stock to make a cylinder *(pages 94–95)* 3 mm greater in diameter than the wide end of the planned taper. Then set the tool rest just above the centre of the stock and 6 mm away from it, turn on the lathe, and mark the ends of the taper with a pencil. If the taper is to be longer than 200 mm, mark its centre as well. Starting at the wide end of the taper, place a parting tool on edge on the tool rest with the lower bevel of the cutting edge against the stock and the tool handle angled slightly downwards. Then raise the handle to drive the cutting edge into the stock.

Stop the lathe frequently so that you can check the depth of the narrow cut, using calipers set to the desired diameter *(inset)*. The cut is completed when both points of the calipers slide easily on to the wood inside the groove. Then cut and measure a groove at the narrow end of the taper in the same manner.

To establish the diameter needed for a middle groove in a taper longer than 200 mm, add the diameters of the end grooves and divide by two.

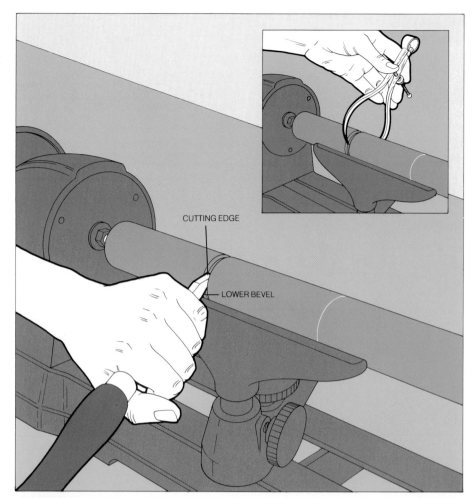

CUTTING EDGE

LOWER BEVEL

2 **Cutting the taper.** Starting at the groove that marks the wide end of the taper, cut along the entire length of the taper with a large gouge. Gradually apply greater forward pressure along the length of the cut, removing more wood as you approach the narrow end. Repeat the same cutting motion until you have reached the desired diameter at both ends of the taper. Stop the lathe periodically and hold a straightedge against the wood, to be sure there are no unwanted bulges.

Use a skew chisel in one continuous cut to smooth the surface of the taper *(page 95)*.

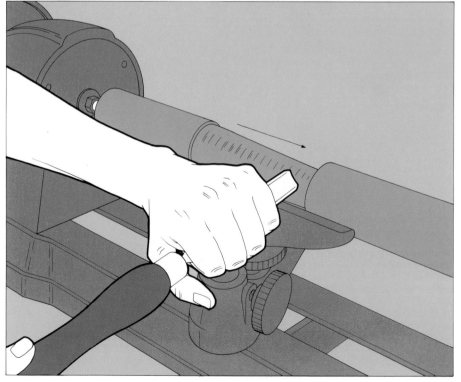

A Rectangular Section with Rounded Shoulders

1 Marking off the rectangle. First square off the entire length of the stock with a table saw and plane or sand the surfaces smooth. Then use a pencil and a combination square to mark the ends of any section that will remain square after the turning is completed. Mark both ends of the section on all four faces of the stock. In the example shown in the drawing below, the rectangle is at the end of the piece of stock, so only one set of pencil lines is necessary. Mount the stock on the lathe as described on page 92, but do not bevel the edges with a plane.

2 Cutting a groove. Set the tool rest level with the centre of the stock, making sure that the edges of the spinning stock will clear the tool rest by 6 mm. Turn on the lathe and set a skew chisel, point down, on the tool rest, with the handle angled slightly downwards. Push the skew point straight into the wood at the guideline. Then roll the tool handle alternately to the left and the right, opening up the cut to form a V-groove about 12 mm wide. Apply forward pressure until the point starts to cut all round the stock. Make the same cut at any other guidelines.

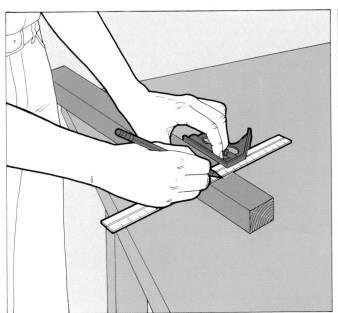

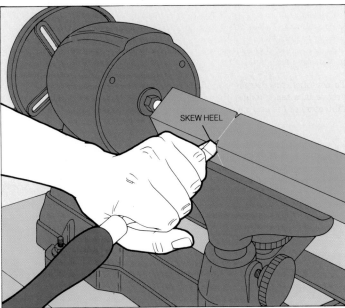

3 Rounding the shoulders. With the wood still spinning, position the skew chisel on the tool rest in line with the V-groove, the skew point on top and angled towards the rectangular section. The cutting edge should be almost horizontal, the skew point well above the spinning corners so that it does not catch and chip the stock. Push the blade forwards and, with a motion similar to the one used to cut the side of a bead *(page 96)*, raise the tool handle with a steady pressure to direct the cutting edge into the wood as you roll the heel of the cutting edge down into the V-groove. End the motion with the cutting edge in a vertical position. Continue to make similar cuts until the shoulder is fully rounded.

If you want to cut a deeper shoulder, use a gouge to remove the excess stock that is adjacent to the shoulder *(page 94)*.

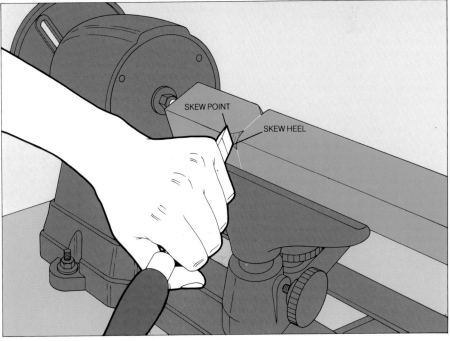

Using a Template to Plan and Turn a Spindle

1 Making the template. Draw an outline of the proposed design parallel to and about 50 mm from the edge of a sheet of heavy paper. Use a ruler to measure the diameters of the breaks—the high and low points of every shape in the design. As you measure each break, draw a line from it to the edge of the paper; on each line, note the diameter of the shape at that point. Note the diameter at the midpoint of any taper longer than 200 mm. If you are duplicating the shape of an existing piece of turned wood, use calipers to measure the break diameters and the spacing between breaks. Then transfer the measurements to the paper.

Glue the paper pattern to a piece of 3 mm hardboard, lining up the paper edge with the hardboard edge. To make the template—actually a reverse pattern of the design—cut along the pattern edge nearest the edge of the hardboard *(inset)*, using a band saw. Then smooth the curves and grooves of the template with a file.

Mount your stock in the lathe and turn it to a cylinder, except in the sections that are projected to remain rectangular *(page 99)*.

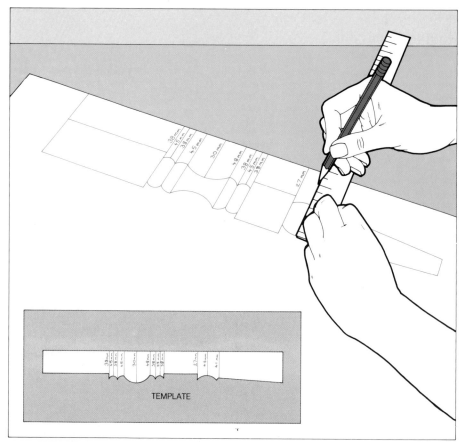

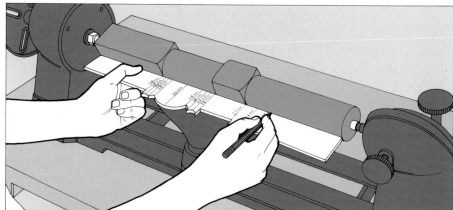

TEMPLATE

2 Marking guidelines on the wood. With the lathe at rest, hold the straight edge of the template against the stock and, at the end of each break line, make a pencil mark on the cylinder. Then remove the template, place the pencil on the tool rest with the point against a mark and rotate the wood by hand to draw a guideline completely round the cylinder. Repeat this procedure at every break point.

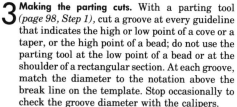

3 Making the parting cuts. With a parting tool *(page 98, Step 1)*, cut a groove at every guideline that indicates the high or low point of a cove or a taper, or the high point of a bead; do not use the parting tool at the low point of a bead or at the shoulder of a rectangular section. At each groove, match the diameter to the notation above the break line on the template. Stop occasionally to check the groove diameter with the calipers.

When all the grooves have been cut to the correct depth, begin to shape the cylinder, using the tools and cutting techniques on pages 94–95.

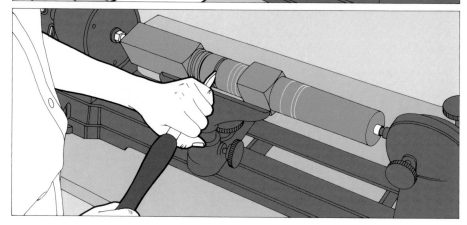

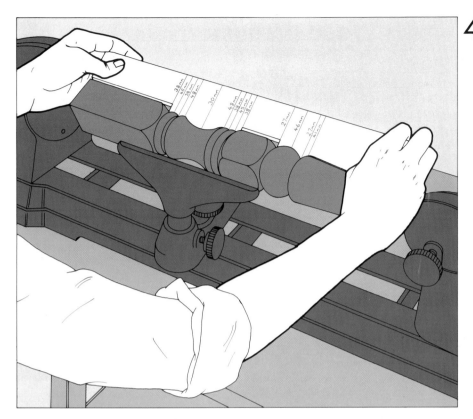

4 **Using the template to check your work.** As you shape the cylinder, stop the lathe periodically and hold the cut edge of the template against your work, noting which sections need additional cutting. The shaping is complete when the template fits snugly against the spindle, with no gaps between the template and the wood.

Smoothing Shaped Wood on a Spinning Lathe

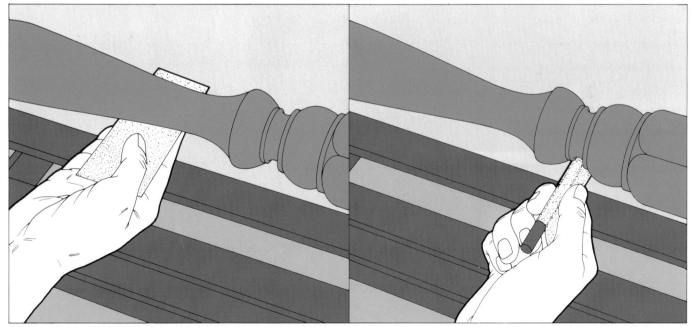

Sanding the spinning stock. To smooth shapes like the elongated taper shown above, left, start with a sheet of 120 grade open-coat garnet paper; fold it in thirds to a width of about 5 cm. Turn on the lathe and hold the paper underneath the spinning stock, pressing lightly and moving steadily back and forth along the shape to avoid sanding away too much wood in one spot. Repeat the procedure with 160 grade paper.

To smooth a narrower shape, such as a V-groove or a small cove *(above, right)*, just wrap the piece of garnet paper around a dowel or a wedge that fits the shape, and hold the paper below the stock as it spins on the lathe. Press the paper lightly against the wood, taking care not to rub away the definition of the shape. Finish with a finer grade of paper, as above.

After you have sanded the stock, apply a coat of special sanding sealer, rub down with very fine steel wool, and apply wax polish or the finish of your choice.

Turning Wood on a Faceplate

Wood-turning on a faceplate—that is, with the wood anchored at only one end of the lathe—is favoured by woodworkers with an eye for exotic grains and a penchant for designing bowls, doorknobs and newel-post caps in unusual shapes.

Some lathes have special features for faceplate turning. On a gap-bed lathe, part of the bed next to the headstock is cut away to leave extra room for a large piece of wood. On some other lathes, the headstock is equipped for outboard turning, which allows the faceplate to be mounted on the outside end of the headstock; this allows larger workpieces to be turned and gives easier access to the work. But an ordinary lathe will shape the face of a piece of wood up to about 20 cm in diameter—wide enough to accommodate, for example, a doorknob or the newel-post cap that is shown on these two pages.

Faceplates that screw on to the headstock spindle and anchor the spinning wood *(page 91)* are available in several sizes; choose one about 12 mm smaller in diameter than the base of the piece that you are planning to turn. The screws that are used to fasten the wood to the faceplate should be as long as possible—up to 50 mm. But be sure that the screws will not extend into a part of the wood that is going to be cut away.

Although cutting tools may be used to round the sides of the wood as it is being turned on a faceplate, the shaping is generally done with scraping tools. Scraping *(page 92, right)* gives greater control over the tool and the spinning stock; this is necessary because the pieces of wood used in faceplate turning are wider, and therefore the outer edges are revolving at greater speeds. Scraping is also the preferred method for the shaping of end grain, an integral part of faceplate turning.

Wood is prepared for faceplate turning much as it is for spindle turning *(page 93, Step 1)*. First square the piece on a table saw, then plane the surface that will be fastened to the faceplate. Draw diagonal lines from corner to corner on the planed surface to locate the centre point of the wood. Then use a compass to draw a circle from the centre point, 3 mm larger than the largest diameter of the finished piece. Use a band saw to trim away excess wood round the outside of the circle.

Mounting and Turning a Newel-Post Cap

1 Fastening the stock to the faceplate. Position the faceplate on the planed surface of the stock, aligning the threaded centre hole of the faceplate with the centre point on the wood. With a pencil, mark the faceplate screw-hole locations on the wood. Drill pilot holes, and screw the faceplate to the stock. Then screw the faceplate to the headstock spindle on the lathe.

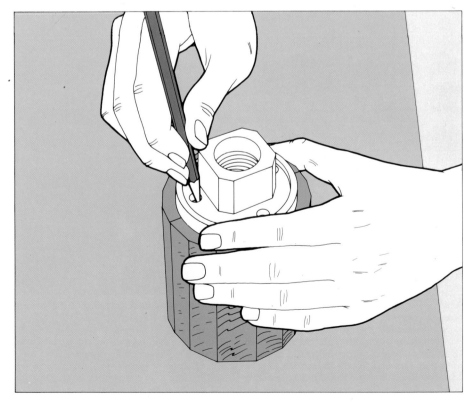

FACEPLATE

2 **Shaping the sides of the cap.** Smooth the wood to a cylinder *(page 94, Steps 1 and 2)*, and use a round-nose chisel to shape the sides of the cap. For a cove shape, set the chisel on the tool rest at the planned centre of the cap, hold the tool in the scraping position *(page 92)*, bevel edge down, and press the cutting edge straight into the spinning wood to make a preliminary groove. Widen the groove to the desired cove shape by repeating the same scraping procedure on either side of the groove, sliding the chisel towards the centre of the cove and increasing the forward pressure as you go along.

To form a bead shape, use a square-nose chisel in the same pivoting motion described in Step 3 *(below)*, forming first one side, then the other.

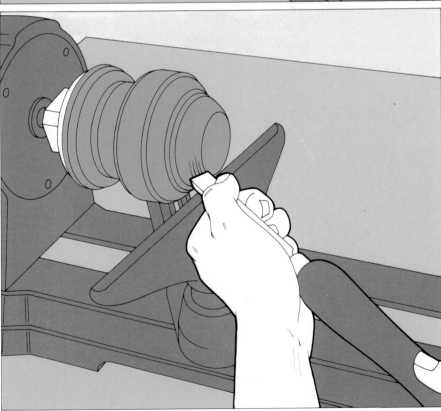

3 **Rounding the end of the cap.** To shape end grain into a convex dome, set the tool rest at about a 45-degree angle to the centre line of the stock and from the wood. Rest a square-nose chisel on the tool rest in the scraping position, bevel down, and push the left corner of the cutting edge into the spinning wood to scrape a shallow groove. Then gradually slide the blade along the tool rest, pivoting the cutting edge in a gentle arc towards the centre of the stock. Take care not to move the tool past the centre of the stock, because of the danger of the tool being thrown upwards by the upward spin of the workpiece. Repeat the scraping motion until the wood is the desired shape, stopping to readjust the tool rest whenever necessary.

Form a groove or a dish-like depression in the end grain with a round-nose chisel, using the scraping technique in Step 2 *(above)*.

High-Speed Sanders for a Perfect Finish

Many woodworking projects are simpler to finish if the parts are sanded before they are assembled, and there are several kinds of power sanders to make quick work of this step. For the serious woodworker who has regular need of a sander, a bench-mounted combination belt-and-disc sander, which smooths both flat surfaces and many that are curved or irregular, is the most appropriate tool to acquire *(below)*. For occasional work, portable sanders provide a less expensive alternative, but tools of this kind will generally be limited to specific uses *(page 107)*.

The continuous abrasive belt of the bench-mounted sander stretches across two rotating drums and can be orientated for the job at hand. Set horizontally, it is especially useful for sanding parallel to the grain and for sanding long boards; if the boards are wider than the belt, they are sanded in repeated passes. Set vertically, the belt is useful for sanding the ends of wide boards, such as those used to construct deep drawers, but you can also adapt it for working on a variety of curved and elongated surfaces.

The disc sander, the other component of this combination tool, is best suited to sanding end grain on smaller pieces of wood; it is also useful for smoothing mitre cuts, bevels and outside curves, such as the edge of a wooden disc. With a belt sander, it is essential to keep the work moving continuously. Power sanding removes a great deal of wood so quickly that holding the work in one place for more than a moment can flatten a curve or put a dimple into a flat surface. Movement also helps keep the abrasive surface from clogging.

Routine care for all power sanders includes inspecting abrasive surfaces frequently, and brushing clogged areas on such surfaces clean. Replace frayed or tearing belts or discs as they can cause injury if they break while in use.

With all power sanders, use only the abrasive discs or belts recommended for the tool. These are usually surfaced with silicone oxide, silicone carbide or garnet, and are available in various different grades for rough or fine sanding. Sandpaper (properly termed glass paper) is not strong enough for high-speed sanding.

A combination belt-and-disc sander. This bench-mounted tool offers two methods of sanding in one machine. The belt sander has a continuous strip of abrasive-coated fabric, usually 50 to 100 mm wide. The belt rotates over two drums: the drive drum, turned by the motor, and the idler drum, which turns freely. A knob on the side of the belt unit adjusts the tracking of the belt, which is released or tightened by a spring handle. The belt unit can be positioned either vertically or horizontally.

The disc sander, which shares the machine's motor with the belt sander, is a circular metal plate to which an abrasive-coated disc is fixed. A detachable worktable can be fitted as required to both the disc and the belt sander. The table can be tilted and locked at any angle for bevelling or for smoothing mitre joints. The table has channels for fences or mitre gauges.

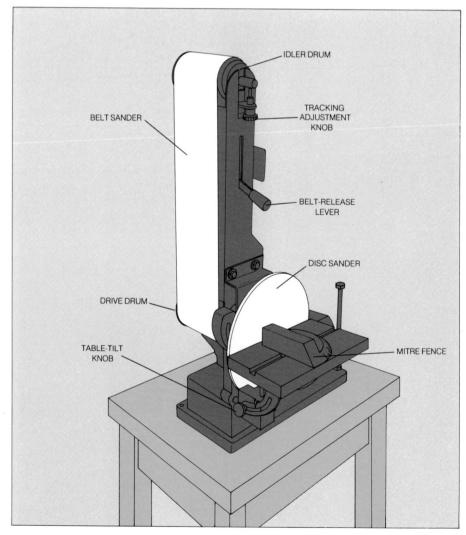

IDLER DRUM

TRACKING ADJUSTMENT KNOB

BELT SANDER

BELT-RELEASE LEVER

DISC SANDER

DRIVE DRUM

MITRE FENCE

TABLE-TILT KNOB

Safety Precautions for Belt Sanders

In addition to the safety rules for all power tools *(page 14)*, observe these precautions for belt sanders:

□ Hold the work with your fingers on the top edge or the upper face of the stock, to avoid sanding your fingertips.

□ When sanding a small object, tack a piece of scrap wood to the back of the object and use it as a gripping block.

□ Feed the work against the rotation of a belt sander, to prevent the work from being pulled off the belt.

□ Hold the work against the downward rotation of a disc sander, to prevent the piece from being lifted off the disc table.

□ Remove all wood dust before sanding metal objects, as metal sanding throws sparks that might ignite the wood dust.

□ Wear goggles and a mask while sanding, and use a vacuum attachment when doing a great deal of sanding.

□ Ensure that any nails or screws in the work are either removed or are well recessed below the surface.

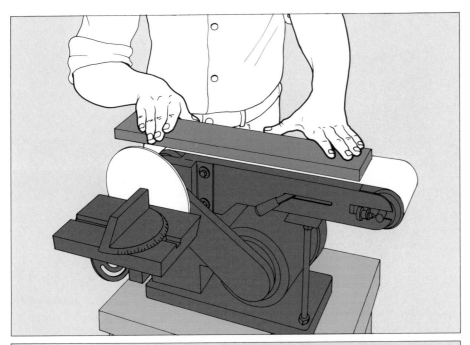

Using a Belt and Disc to Sand Flat Surfaces

Sanding a lengthwise surface. Remove the belt table, and lock the belt unit in a horizontal position. With the motor on, grip the board with your left hand and feed it on to the belt with your right hand, against the rotation of the belt. Keep the grain parallel to the belt, moving the board along the length of the belt in a continuous motion, with a light, even pressure. Make repeated passes over the belt until the surface is smooth.

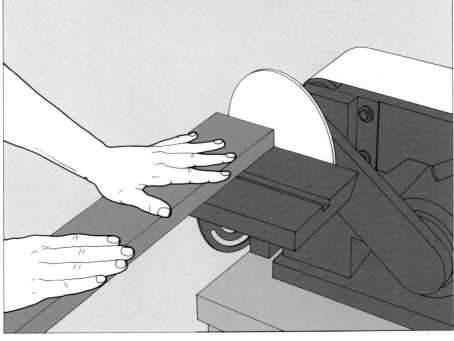

Sanding ends. For a square end, position the disc table horizontally, using a try square to set it perpendicular to the sanding disc. With the motor on, hold the end of the board against the left side of the disc, on the downward side of the rotation, and move it back and forth between the left edge and the centre of the disc, maintaining light, continuous pressure. Use a mitre gauge, if necessary, to keep the wood flush against the disc.

To sand a bevelled end, set the disc table at the desired angle, using a sliding bevel to match the angles of disc and board. Sand the bevel as you would a square end, moving it between the left edge and the centre of the disc.

Adapting the Belt Sander to Curved Surfaces

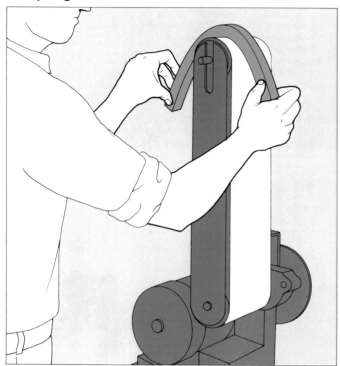

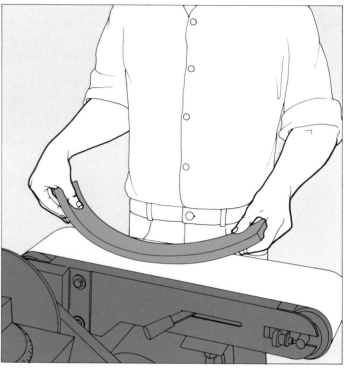

Sanding an inside curve. With the belt sander locked in a vertical position, turn on the motor and gently pass the inside of the curved piece over the belt at the idler drum, against the rotation of the belt. Maintain a light, even pressure and a continuous motion. At the completion of each pass, return to the starting point; repeat until you are satisfied with the finish.

Sanding an outside curve. Lock the belt unit in a horizontal position and turn on the motor. Holding the curved piece at each end, rock it in a series of arcs against the belt, following the curve of the piece. Apply even pressure in order to remove an equal amount of waste along the whole length of the piece.

Particular Uses for Portable Sanders

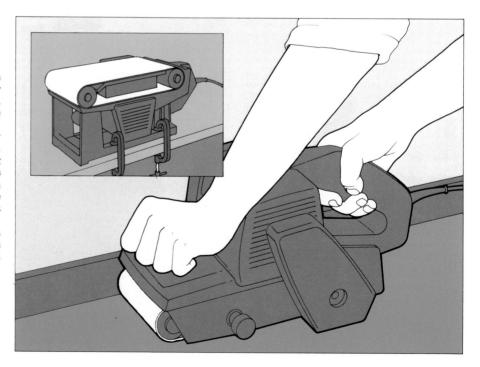

A portable belt sander. Fitted with abrasive belts varying from coarse to fine, a portable belt sander is used to remove surface waste from floorboards, doors and other work that cannot practicably be brought to the bench.

Switch on the machine, then lower it carefully to the work and keep it moving along the grain. Hold the machine firmly to prevent it running away, but do not apply any downward pressure as the sander will work effectively under its own weight. Take special care with veneers, where the fast action of the belt can result in sanding right through the thin layer of wood.

To convert the portable belt sander into a stationary bench model, secure it upside down in a special stand *(inset)* which is supplied as an accessory by the manufacturer.

A disc sander. Widely used for preparatory work, this power drill attachment is inexpensive and effective but tends to dig into wood and leave whirls on the surface that are difficult to remove.

The face of the flexible disc must be kept at an angle of about 30 degrees to the work. Switch on the drill, depress the disc to bring a section of it into contact with the wood, and move the sander continuously backwards and forwards so that only a thin skim of the surface is removed. Hold the drill with both hands to maintain the disc at the proper angle.

An orbital sander. Orbital or finishing sanders are obtainable as attachments to power drills or as integral tools with their own built-in motors. Designed for fine-sanding large flat surfaces both across and with the grain, they work with a vibrating movement that oscillates backwards, forwards and sideways.

Switch on the machine before lowering the full face of the sander on to the workpiece, then move it slowly to and fro in long strokes. Do not apply downward pressure—this will clog the abrasive sheet with waste, and could cause it to tear and score the wood.

A flap wheel. This power drill attachment consists of a large number of abrasive cloth strips attached radially to a central hub, and is designed to sand internal curves and sharp corners that cannot be reached by orbital, belt or disc sanders. Flap wheels are available in different diameters and with different grades of abrasive surfaces.

Advance the flap wheel carefully towards the work until the outer edge of the revolving leaves is brushing against the surface. Do not apply any pressure with the tool. To sand intricate or inaccessible areas, it may be necessary to approach the work from several different angles.

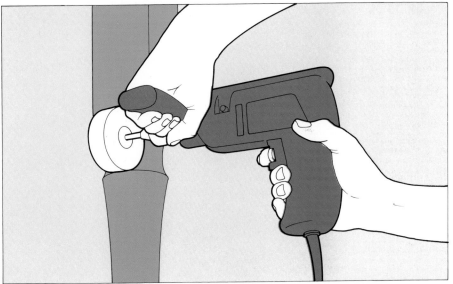

4 Skin-Deep Beauty with Veneers

An inlaid border for a tabletop. Strips of patterned banding set into a mahogany tabletop create in a short time a decorative effect that once took hours of deft and painstaking craftsmanship. The inlays, which come in dozens of styles, are cut to length with a trimming knife, then glued into a router-cut groove.

To a poet, veneer is a symbol of shallow deceit, a false front of beauty that inevitably falls away to reveal some kind of evil. To a craftsman, veneer is a thin layer of wood that turns a plain board into a beautiful one. But it also does much more. It is wood that does things no other kind of wood can do. Veneer makes plain boards stronger and more resistant to warping. It hides joints and makes them stronger, too. More important, veneer liberates the craftsman to display the grain of wood in ways that are economically, structurally or physically impossible with solid timber.

Though veneer is almost as fragile as an eggshell and is produced from wood that is treated with steam or soaked in boiling water to soften it before it is cut, the machinery that makes it is anything but delicate. Rotary equipment can take the form of a giant lathe with a single blade as wide as the log is long. The motor that spins the log sends the veneers pouring forth from the surface of the log in the form of one immense shaving. A second type of rotary machine holds a half-round log against a rotating shaft. With each rotation the log is brought a little closer to the blade, and a slice of veneer is peeled off in an arc gentler than the arcs of the growth rings. Because the wood is cut on a curve, rotary equipment gives grain effects that would be impossible to achieve with flat boards. The method creates a grain pattern that magnifies the width of the rings—more so when the veneer is cut from the full log than in half-round cutting.

An especially fine veneer—often used for round tabletops—is made using a radial cutting machine, which works like a pencil sharpener to cut an endless strip of veneer conically from the end of a trunk.

Reciprocating machines work something like the meat slicer in a butcher's shop. The wood stock—a squared-off log called a flitch—is attached to a moving plate and driven past a fixed blade that peels off a slice at a time. As the sheets come off the machine they are numbered and stacked in order so that woodworkers can make use of the mirror-image grain patterns that once-adjacent surfaces present. Sometimes the flitch is first cut in quarters lengthwise, to yield grain patterns like those of quarter-sawed boards. Reciprocating machines can slice up otherwise useless parts of a tree—and with spectacular results. For instance, injured areas, too unstable for most woodworking, give an exquisite, rolling pattern called burr.

Because the veneer-making process uses wood so efficiently, consuming virtually every part of the tree, the expensive pursuit of exotic woods becomes worthwhile. More than 200 varieties of wood are available, each one sliced up with something of the diamond cutter's sensibility, for a bountiful harvest of beauty that is less than a millimetre deep. To the woodworker, that is deep enough.

Gluing a Thin Coat of Wood Over a Solid Base

The art of veneering—layering a thin skin of decorative wood over a common wood—was once practised only by master craftsmen. But modern glues and improved techniques for cutting veneers from raw logs have changed all that. Now a home craftsman, working with a small kit of special tools, can achieve delightful transformations in the surfaces of furniture, doors, and even architectural trim. Many of the necessary tools, as well as the other materials used in veneering, can normally be found at local timberyards and hardware stores, although some items may have to be specially ordered.

Most of the veneers produced today are sliced from half-round sections of tree trunk or from squared-off logs called flitches. High-precision blades slice the wood into sheets 0.5 to 1.5 mm thick. The sheets are stacked flat in the sequence in which they are sliced, their edges are generally left untrimmed and they are priced by the square metre.

In addition to taking veneers from the tree trunk, manufacturers also make use of parts of the tree normally considered waste wood—the roots, burrs, stumps and crotches that are too unstable for construction. These waste woods yield veneers with exotic grain patterns and colourings, from the whirling spirals of burrs to the V-shaped grain of crotch wood—taken from a section where a major limb branches out from the trunk.

So distinctive are some of these grain patterns that the tree species is instantly recognizable. Walnut, elm and maple, for example, are notable for their flamboyant burr and stump-wood patterns, rosewood and zebrawood for their distinctive varicoloured stripes, oak and mahogany for their rippling grain. Matched sections of these patterned veneers produce designs that seem almost three-dimensional.

Applying veneer can be done in several ways, but the process always begins with a flattening procedure. This step is often carried out by the veneer supplier. To flatten highly patterned woods, which tend to be brittle and wavy, each sheet of veneer is dampened with a sponge until it is saturated but not sodden. Then the sheet is pressed between two pieces of plywood; cramps are used to increase the pressure gradually as the veneer dries. When the wood is only slightly clammy to the touch, it is ready to use.

For large surfaces, such as doors and tabletops, the best way to apply veneer is to glue and clamp it to the base. Usually the veneer is applied in sections, and adjacent sections must be perfectly spliced, so that the gap between them is almost indiscernible. To make such a joint, the edges which will adjoin are trimmed with a trimming knife or with a scalpel.

Veneer pins are used to hold the sections of veneer in place temporarily; these pins have needle-like points that leave nearly invisible holes. Later, when the sections are glued down, gummed paper tape holds the spliced edges together until the glue dries. This tape, which has a water-soluble backing, is preferable to masking tape, which might lift veneer slivers when you come to remove it.

Clamping, which ensures a tight bond between the veneer and the base, is also an important step in veneering. The pressure exerted by clamping should bear down directly and evenly on the surface beneath. This kind of clamping is best done with a caul—a piece of chipboard or plywood at least 19 mm thick with battens and cross-braces clamped over it to distribute the pressure evenly.

On curved surfaces, such as those on rounded cabinet fronts, it is virtually impossible to achieve uniform pressure by clamping. For such jobs, the preferred method of pressing the veneer against the base is a technique called hammer veneering, which uses no clamps at all. Instead, the veneer is pressed smooth against the glued surface with a spade-shaped tool called a veneer hammer. Traditionally, hammer veneering relied on hide glue, which had to be heated, and hard-earned skill; but today, modern glues simplify the job and produce good results.

A third veneering method uses contact adhesive, which bonds instantly and also requires no clamping. But instant bonding creates problems because it allows no corrections. Contact adhesive is best reserved for veneering small areas, such as the edges of tables and shelves.

Regardless of the method used, to be successful, veneering must be carefully planned. The base should be a stable surface, such as chipboard or fibreboard. On solid wood, splinters should be smoothed away and holes filled with epoxy filler.

If you are working with stock less than 25 mm thick, prepare to veneer both surfaces as otherwise the piece may warp. The grain of veneer should always run parallel to the grain of solid wood but at right angles to the grain of plywood.

As you work, keep your tools close at hand so that you do not have to hunt for them just as the glue is freshly spread. Be prepared for repairs—but do not attempt to make them until the glue has dried. Highly figured veneers may need patching, cracks may develop along the grain, and sections of veneer may even lift and need to be reglued and reclamped. When the job is complete, finish the veneer just as you would solid wood, with stains and French polish, or a cellulose-based finish.

Pair-Bonded Veneers

Combining veneers for effect. Consecutive sheets of veneer cut from a flitch are nearly identical in pattern but can be arranged to create completely dissimilar designs. Two sheets, opened as if they were pages of a book, present a mirror image and are called book-matched veneer; you can extend book-matching over large surfaces by flipping over every second sheet. Sheets laid just as they come from the stack, in a repeating pattern, are called slip-matched; this pattern is most effective with long narrow sheets cut from narrow flitches.

Veneers with very straight grain lend themselves well to a diamond arrangement, or to a variation in which the diamond shape is reversed so that the grain of the wood radiates from a central point. For either of these patterns, start by cutting four identical rectangles of veneer, with the grain running diagonally across each of the rectangles. Then position the rectangles edge to edge, forming either a pattern of concentric diamonds or a pattern of radiating lines.

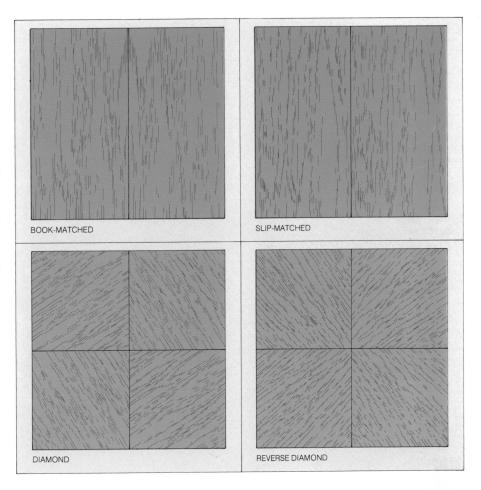

BOOK-MATCHED

SLIP-MATCHED

DIAMOND

REVERSE DIAMOND

Virtues and Failings of Veneering Glues

□ WHITE PVA GLUE is an inexpensive, water-soluble adhesive that takes four to six hours to harden. This slow set-up time is an advantage in veneering large areas, because it allows alignments to be perfected before the new surface is locked in place. White glue does require extensive clamping, however, and once the job is finished the veneer must always be protected from moisture or it will lift away from its base. Apply white glue with a paint roller, a brush or a comb-type glue spreader. When you are using white glue with highly figured veneers, which warp when exposed to water, spread glue on the base surface only. Clean white glue from tools in warm water.

□ UREA FORMALDEHYDE RESIN is more waterproof than white glue, but is less convenient to work with. It comes in powder form and has to be mixed with water, then applied with a brush to both the base and the back of the veneer. Take care not to get the glue on an exposed surface, as it will stain the finish. Slide the veneer into position and clamp it firmly. Unlike white glue, urea formaldehyde can take up to 24 hours to dry completely, but tools should be cleaned in water immediately after use.

□ CONTACT ADHESIVE bonds instantly and thus needs no clamping, but it does not allow corrections once the veneer is positioned. Use a serrated spatula to spread the adhesive evenly on both the veneer and the base. Let it dry for five to 15 minutes, or until it no longer feels sticky when touched with a finger. Then carefully press the veneer in place with your fingers and a roller. Use cellulose thinner to remove drips and to clean your tools after use. Keep the workplace well ventilated as contact adhesives can give off toxic fumes.

□ HIDE GLUE, made from the hide and hooves of animals, has been the classic glue for veneering for centuries. It is sold as a powder or small pearls to be mixed with water. The advantage of hide glue is that it dries at room temperature to make a durable bond but softens under heat, simplifying minor adjustments and repairs. But it must be heated during use and kept within the narrow range of 54° to 64°C. Today, most woodworkers avoid the inconvenience of a heated gluepot and heated metal tools, and opt for a more modern glue instead.

□ IRON-ON VENEER STRIPS are coated on one side with hot-melt glue and are available in most woods up to 300 mm wide. The strips are placed on the base, then pressed with a household iron set at LOW. They can be cut to shape with a trimming knife and are quick and convenient for small areas, but they produce a less durable bond than the more conventional forms of adhesive and are not water-resistant.

Splicing and Clamping Large Veneer Surfaces

1 **Splicing adjoining sheets.** Arrange sheets of veneer in the desired grain pattern, with their joining edges overlapped by 10 mm and their outside edges protruding 5 mm beyond the edges of the base. Clamp a metal straightedge along the line to be spliced and, using a trimming knife, cut through both sheets at once. Slice in short strokes along the guide, to prevent the thin blade from following the curve of the grain.

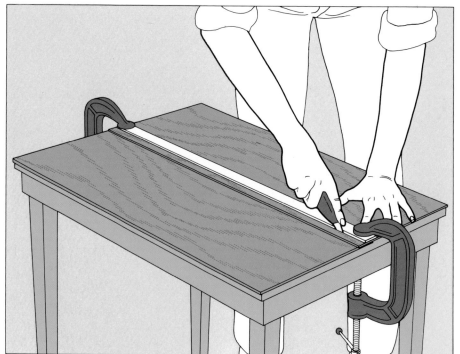

2 **Spreading the glue.** To coat both veneer and base with glue, lay the veneer face down on a work surface covered with newspaper; use a small paint roller to spread glue thickly and evenly to the edges. To prevent the veneer from shifting and excess glue from smearing its face, hold the sheets steady with a bradawl or an old screwdriver. Roll glue on to the base in the same manner, wiping off any drips with a rag.

Lay the veneer on the base, matching the grain patterns along the seam line and maintaining an even 5 mm overlap at the edges of the base. Press and smooth the surface with your hands, shifting the veneer sections slightly to close any gaps in the seam. Then secure the sheets with veneer pins spaced 150 mm apart and about 75 mm from the seam line.

3 **Rolling the veneer.** Use a wallpaper-seam roller to press out air pockets and excess glue from between the veneer and the base. Push the roller from the centre of the base towards its edges, wiping off the extruded glue as you go. Roll along the seam to press it flat.

Secure the spliced edges by covering the seam with paper tape. Cut a piece of tape the same length as the seam and dampen it with a sponge, then smooth it in place along the seam. At 300 mm intervals, fasten additional 100 mm strips of tape across the seam. Remove the pins.

4 **Clamping the work.** To apply uniform pressure to the veneered surface, cover it with a caul held in place by clamped cross-braces. Cut the caul from plywood or chipboard, making it large enough to protrude 10 mm beyond the edges of the veneered surface. To prevent the caul from becoming glued to the veneer when pressure is applied, cover the veneer with wax paper. Then lift the caul gently on to the veneer; take care not to shift the veneer, because the glue will still be soft.

Place 50 by 25 mm battens along the caul, spaced at 150 mm intervals, then position 100 by 50 mm cross-braces on edge across the battens at 400 mm intervals, slipping a scrap piece of veneer beneath the centre of each brace to increase the pressure at the centre of the caul. Tighten cramps on the centre cross-brace first, so that glue will be forced from the centre of the caul towards its edges. Wipe off any excess glue, and continue tightening the cross-brace until no more glue appears. Then tighten cramps on the end cross-braces.

Let the glue dry for 12 hours. Remove the cramps and the caul, and peel off the wax paper.

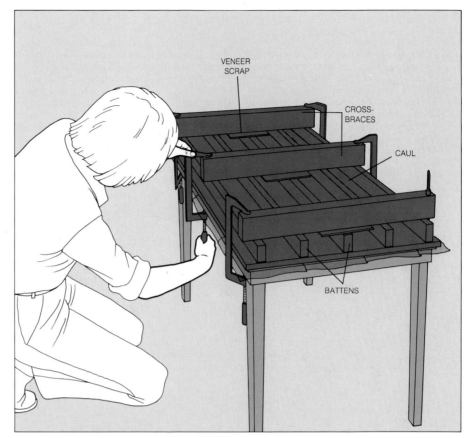

5 **Trimming the edges.** Using the caul to protect your worktable, turn the veneered surface upside down and trim off the protuding veneer with a trimming knife. Start at a corner and cut along the edge to within a few centimetres of the next corner. Then turn the blade and cut in the opposite direction, to prevent the fragile corners of the veneer from being torn off.

When all of the edges have been trimmed, set the veneered surface right side up; dampen the paper tape with a sponge, then remove it. Sand away any residual glue or tape.

A Time-Honoured Method for Veneering Over Curves

Two veneer hammers. Both the professional's veneer hammer *(below, left)* and the home-made veneer hammer *(below, right)* have smooth metal blades designed to press veneer against a curved base. The shop-bought version has a hardwood handle with a spade-shaped metal head, 85 mm wide; the upper end of the head is used as a grip, for bearing down on the veneer. The simple and inexpensive home-made veneer hammer works like a squeegee. The handle is a 19 mm dowel, 275 mm long, filed down at one end; it fits into a socket drilled at the centre of the hardwood head. The two parts are secured with glue and a 25 mm screw. The head, which is cut from 12 mm stock, is 85 mm long by 60 mm wide. The plate is made of 6 mm thick brass or aluminium plate, set to protrude 6 mm beyond the bottom edge of the head. Its working edge is filed smooth and its corners are rounded, to stop them from gouging or scratching the veneer. Matching holes are drilled through the plate and the head, and the two are fastened together with bolts and wing nuts, making the plate detachable for cleaning. Caution: do not use iron or steel for the plate. Either metal could react with the tannic acid present in most woods and leave stains on the surface of the veneer.

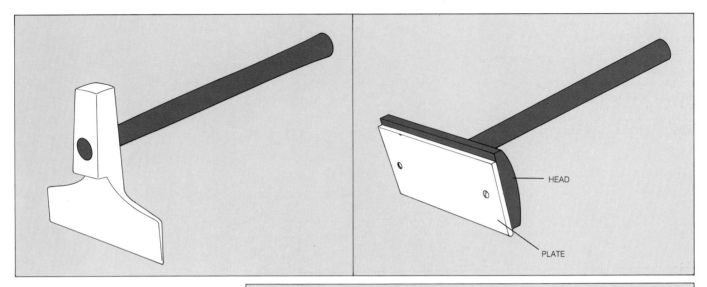

HEAD

PLATE

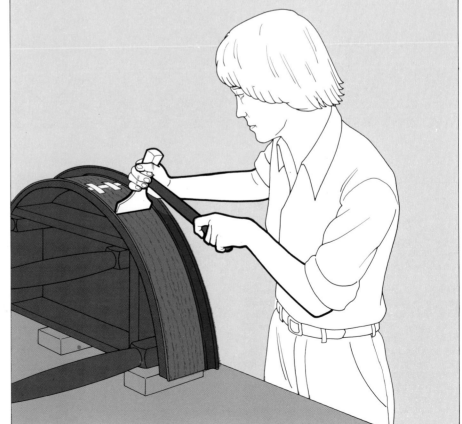

Using the veneer hammer. After laying the glued veneer against the base, smooth it with a hammer, forcing out excess glue and flattening any air pockets. Then bear down with considerable weight, pressing against the head of the hammer, and stroke repeatedly along the veneer in the direction of the grain. Do not work across the grain; this might separate the glue-soaked wood fibres, causing the veneer to crack as it dries.

When using a veneer hammer on spliced veneers, tape the sections together before you glue them on. Work over the taped veneers as if they were a single continuous sheet. Take off the tape only after the glue has dried overnight.

Deflating an Air Pocket

1 **Piercing the veneer.** If an air pocket develops after the glue has hardened, determine its dimensions by tapping on the surface with a fingernail; it will make a dry, hollow sound. Using a trimming knife, make a slit down the middle of the air pocket, following the veneer grain to make the repair less obtrusive. Lift the cut edges of veneer with a palette knife, then gently use the trimming knife to scrape away the old glue from the veneer and the base beneath; blow out the dried glue particles. If the edges are too stiff to bend easily, dampen them with a sponge.

Insert fresh white glue underneath the flaps, using either a glue injector or a small artist's brush. Then roll the veneer flat and wipe away the excess glue as in Step 3, page 112.

2 **Pressing the repair.** To shorten the glue's drying time and stop edges of veneer from lifting, press the repaired area with a household iron set at LOW (65° to 75°C). First cover the repaired area with a piece of wax paper to prevent sticking, and a folded cloth to protect the veneer from scorching. Then press the iron against the area for 30 seconds; check to see if the glue is holding down the veneer edges, and repeat as necessary until the glue is hard. Sand the repair lightly, following the grain of the veneer.

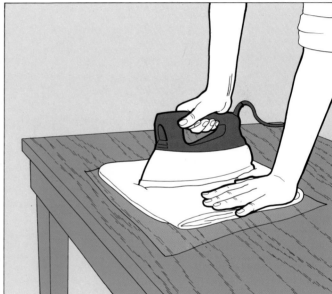

Grafting a Matching Patch

Shaping the patch. Cut away the splintered edges of a veneer split, leaving a clean outline; then make a pattern of the damaged area by placing a piece of paper over the outline and rubbing it with a blunt pencil *(right)*. Use the pattern to cut a patch from veneer that matches as closely as possible the grain and colour of the veneer surrounding the split. Spread the patch with white glue, insert it in the split, and roll it flat. Wipe away the excess glue, and press the patch with a warm iron as in Step 2, above.

Splicing a Decorative Band on to a Veneered Surface

1 **Slicing the banding seams.** Lap the banding veneer over one edge of the veneered surface, and let it overhang that surface slightly. Clamp a straightedge along what will be the seam line between the two pieces of veneer, and slice through both layers at once. Repeat along the other edges of the veneered surface, numbering and marking each banding piece to record its position and seam line. Position the banding along each edge in such a way that its grain runs either parallel or at right angles to the edge of the veneered surface.

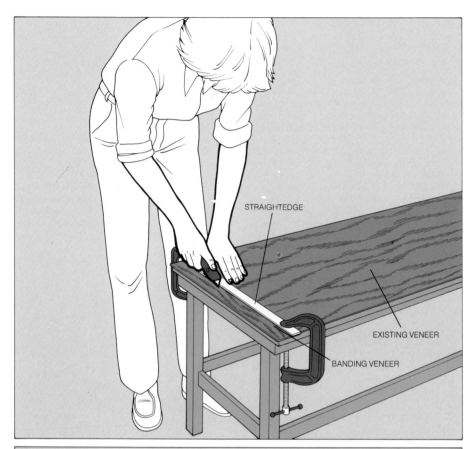

STRAIGHTEDGE

EXISTING VENEER

BANDING VENEER

2 **Removing the existing veneer.** Clamp the straightedge along the seam line of the veneered surface, and prise off the edge of the veneer with a chisel, held bevel down *(right)*. Press down on the straightedge as you work, to avoid damaging the veneer inside the seam line. If the edge of the veneer does crack, repair it before proceeding. Remove the veneer from the other edges, and scrape the dried glue from the cleared areas.

Using paper tape that has water-soluble gum, fasten the pieces of banding in place, matching the seam lines and overlapping the ends of the banding at each corner. Trim the overlapping ends into neatly spliced mitres, using either a wide chisel *(inset)* or a trimming knife and a straightedge. When all the pieces have been cut to fit, dampen the paper tape and remove it.

With a serrated spatula, spread an even coating of contact adhesive on the back of a banding piece and on the cleared edges. When the contact adhesive has cured, lay overlapping strips of wax paper, about 150 mm wide, over the adhesive-covered edge of the panel.

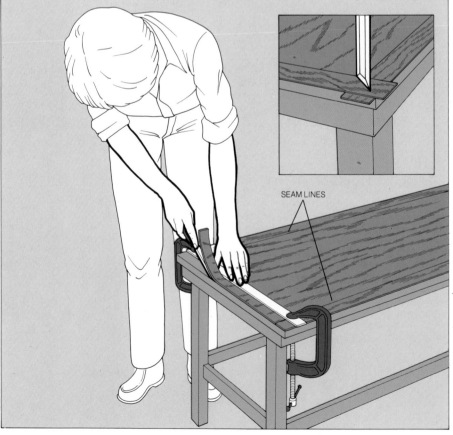

SEAM LINES

3 Setting the banding. Lay the banding over the wax paper and, starting at a corner, slowly pull away the strips of wax paper one at a time, each time pressing the veneer against the exposed edge. Then flatten the banding with a roller. Install the other banding sections in the same way, being especially careful to fit the mitred ends together precisely.

4 Trimming the banding. Using a block plane with its blade set for a very shallow cut, shave away the overlapping edges of banding. Hold the plane with its sole flush to the edge and slide it forwards with short strokes, to avoid pulling away chips of veneer. Plane until the veneer is flush with the edge of the base.

Applying Veneer Edging

Rolling the edgings on. To veneer a vertical edge, either cut your own edging or buy edging tape in the appropriate width, and apply it with contact adhesive and a roller. If you cut your own edging, align the grain to run lengthwise along the side. Lay on the adhesive in a thin coat, so that the line where the edging veneer meets the surface veneer will be less noticeable.

When the adhesive spread on the two adjoining surfaces has cured, start at one corner and position the edging with one hand as you press it smooth with the roller. If necessary, trim the edging at the next corner for a precise fit, before attaching edging to the adjoining side. Once you have attached all the edging strips, gently rub down their edges with fine abrasive paper as this will lessen the possibility of chipping.

Highlighting a Surface with Inlaid Designs

Usually applied over the entire surface of a less attractive base, veneer can also be set into a recess cut into the surface. This technique, called inlaying, is used to highlight a beautifully grained piece of wood or to make an ordinary one more interesting. And though natural or coloured wood veneers are the most common material for inlays, bone, ivory and mother-of-pearl are often used as well.

Inlays take many forms. The most elaborate probably is marquetry, which is made up of small chips, often of different colours and irregular shapes, assembled like a mosaic to form a symbol or a picture. Another form, parquetry, uses small, straight-edged chips to form geometric patterns. Border strips are a form that combines long straight pieces with tiny chips to make narrow ribbon-like patterns. These intricate designs are usually put together first, then inlaid as a unit into a recess cut exactly to fit. Designs made of larger pieces of veneer may be assembled directly in the recess, however, using the same technique as that used to cut and fit adjoining veneer sheets *(page 12)*.

The crucial first step in inlaying is making the recess, which must have a consistent depth and must match the outline of the insert exactly. When you are working on solid wood, a plunging router is an excellent tool for the first part of this job—removing the bulk of the waste from the recess. You will also need a chisel for squaring corners and, when working on designs with intricate outlines, a trimming knife for cutting around the perimeter and some chisels and gouges for clearing the waste from crevices. When you cut a recess into a veneered surface, you first cut the perimeter with a trimming knife, then remove the waste from the recessed area with a chisel *(page 116)*.

Although you can make inlay inserts yourself, a variety of ready-made patterns of many sizes and shapes is available from woodworking suppliers. These inserts are usually packed with a piece of brown paper glued to the finish face and with the insert set into a piece of scrap veneer to protect its edges. Carefully cut away this excess veneer before inlaying the insert, but leave the brown paper in position until after the insert is glued down; sand the paper off during the finishing.

Most inserts are supplied in thicknesses between 0.6 and 0.8 mm. Border strips are available in 1 metre lengths and in widths ranging from about 1 to 12 mm. Because supposedly identical border designs may vary slightly from lot to lot, it is best to order a few extra strips for each project so that, if you need to patch or correct previous work, you can match it exactly.

If you decide to make your own inlays, you can add variety by colouring or shading the veneer you use. Colourfast fabric dyes, mixed with one-quarter the amount of water called for in the instructions, are good for tinting veneers of such light-coloured absorbent woods as poplar or holly. By dipping only the edge of the veneer into the dye, you can obtain a colour gradation with the darkest tone at the edge, where the veneer touches the dye. You can also use ink to colour veneer, either by soaking, or by applying the ink to the veneer with a pen or a brush.

To shade the natural wood on the edge of any kind of veneer—to get a three-dimensional effect—dip the edge into a tray of fine sand, heated over a burner. The scorching of the veneer will be darkest at the point dipped deepest into the sand. In using colouring or shading techniques, always make the veneer a little darker than the final colour or shade actually desired, since finish sanding will remove the darkest surface layer.

Using Strips of Inlay to Form a Border

1 **Routing a straight groove.** Outline the groove needed for the inlay, and fit a plunging router with a bit appropriate to the groove's width. Measure the distance from the outside of the groove to the edge of the workpiece and set the router fence to this distance. Measure the distance from the perimeter of the bit to the edge of the router base; clamp two pieces of 100 by 50 mm timber this distance from the ends of the groove to act as stops at the end of the run. Set the bit to a cutting depth slightly less than the thickness of the inlay and butt the router base against the left-hand stop with the fence pressed to the front of the workpiece. Switch on the router and work along the workpiece from left to right. At the end of the cut, raise the bit and switch the machine off.

If the groove outline is wider than the router bit, reposition the fence as often as needed until all unrouted stock between the groove outlines has been removed. When such a groove turns a corner, finish all passes on one side before proceeding to the adjacent side.

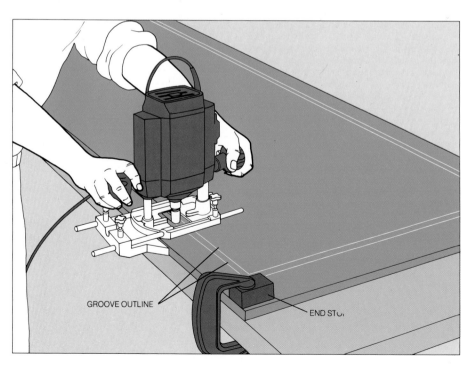

GROOVE OUTLINE

END STOP

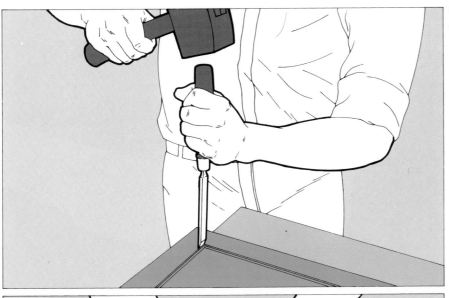

2 **Squaring corners of a routed groove.** Position a sharp, wide wood chisel over the uncut area at the outer corner of the groove, aligning the flat side of the blade with the edge of the groove. Tap the chisel lightly with a mallet. Make an identical cut on the other side of the outer corner, then use the chisel to undercut the waste in the corner. Clean any splinters from the edge of the groove with a trimming knife.

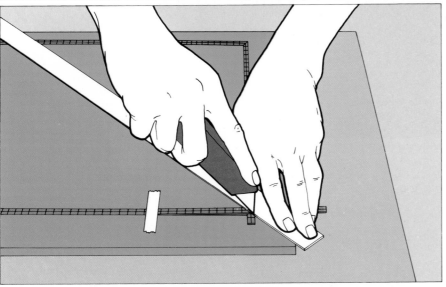

3 **Fitting the inlay in the groove.** Lay the inlay border strips in the grooves so that the patterns match where the strips overlap at the corners. Secure each strip about 50 mm from each corner, with paper tape that has water-soluble gum. Then lay a metal straightedge diagonally across the corner; use a trimming knife to cut a 45-degree mitre through both pieces of inlay, starting at the outside corner and working in.

With grooves too long for a single inlay strip, lay as many in each groove as necessary. Allow about 25 mm of overlap between strips, matching the patterns at the overlap; try to arrange the overlaps so that they occur at regular intervals. Match the corner patterns as well, securing and mitring them as above. Then use the straightedge and the trimming knife to cut through the overlaps along the groove, cutting across the strips at a 90-degree angle.

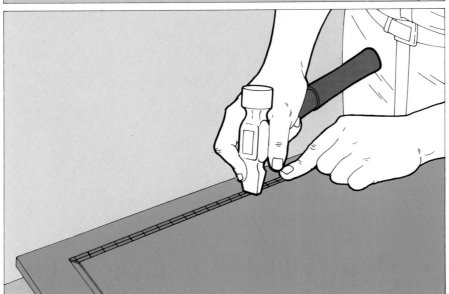

4 **Gluing the border strips.** Spread a thin coat of white glue on the back of each inlay strip, and then return the strips to their grooves. Use the pein of a cross-pein hammer to press the strips firmly into the grooves, making sure that each one is properly aligned before pressing it into place. Wipe away any excess glue with a damp cloth. Cover all of the glued inlay with wax paper; then lay a piece of hardboard, plywood or chipboard over the entire surface, and clamp it or weight it down with heavy objects.

Cutting a Recess for a Small Medallion

1 Preparing the template. Cut a piece of 12 mm plywood to the same size as the workpiece surface, and place the inlay in the desired position on the plywood. Set a pair of sharp dividers 5 mm apart; holding the inlay firmly in place, scribe round it on to the plywood to make an outline 5 mm larger than the original. Remove the inlay and drill a small hole inside the outline on the plywood. Then, using a jigsaw, cut round the scribed outline.

INLAY

2 Cutting the recess. Align the plywood template exactly over the workpiece and secure it with cramps. Attach a 15 mm straight carbide bit to a plunging router, and fit a collar to the base plate to give a 5 mm gap between the outside of the collar and the bit. Adjust the bit to cut slightly less than the thickness of the inlay. Press the collar firmly against the edge of the inlay cutout, then switch on the router, depress the bit and guide the router round the inside of the cutout. After completing the cut round the edge of the template, move the router across the cutout from side to side to remove the remaining waste. Raise the bit and switch off the machine.

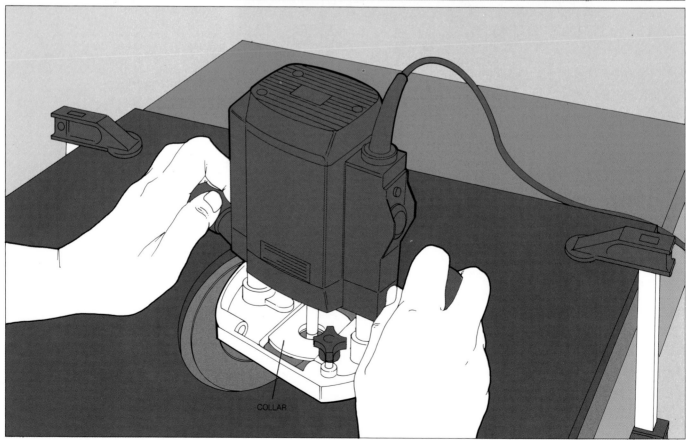

COLLAR

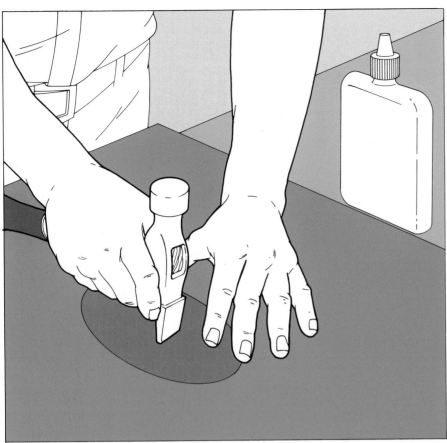

3 **Attaching the inlay.** Spread a thin coat of white glue over the recessed area, and carefully lower the inlay into the recess, brown paper facing up. Use the pein of a cross-pein hammer to smooth the inlay down, working from the centre outwards to force out the excess glue. Secure the edges temporarily with pieces of paper tape.

4 **Clamping the insert.** Cover the inlay with a sheet of wax paper, to prevent excess glue from sticking to the cramp assembly; then cover the inlaid area with a piece of 12 mm plywood or hardboard slightly larger than the area of the inlay. Place two 100 by 50 mm braces on edge at the sides of the plywood, and clamp the ends of the braces to the edge of the work surface.

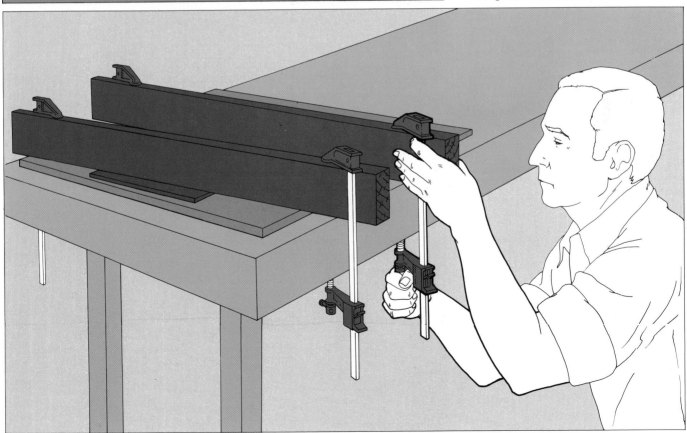

Routing Out a Large Area for a Sizeable Inlay

1 Laying out the area. Mark the desired position for the inlay on the surface of the workpiece, then use a pencil and a straightedge to draw an outline 5 mm larger round it. If the inlay is curved, use a sharp pair of dividers to scribe the outer line *(page 120, Step 1)*.

2 Making the template. Cut a piece of 12 mm plywood 150 mm wide and 50 mm longer than the width of the workpiece. Nail a batten 150 mm long by 50 mm square to one end of the plywood, then hook the plywood over the workpiece. Using a straightedge, mark across the ends of the plywood where it crosses the outer lines on the workpiece. Mark two more lines down the length of the plywood 50 mm in from the sides to complete a long rectangle 50 mm wide. Remove the plywood from the workpiece and cut out the rectangle with a jigsaw.

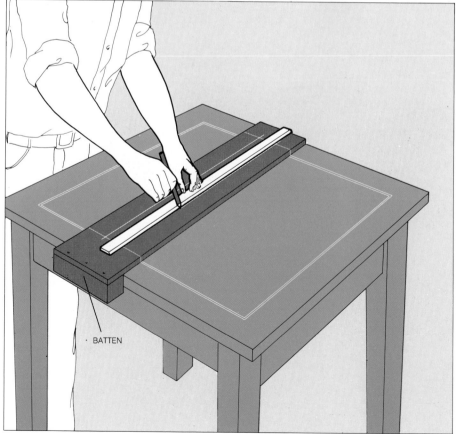

BATTEN

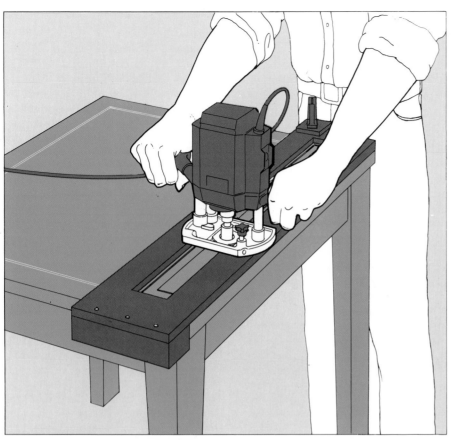

3 **Routing the first section.** Align one long side of the rectangular cutout in the template with the left-hand side of the outline on the workpiece. Make sure that the batten is butted firmly against the workpiece edge, then clamp the template in position. Using the same size bit and collar as in Step 2, page 120, rout along all four sides of the rectangular cutout, then remove the waste in the centre by routing from side to side. Raise the bit and switch off the router.

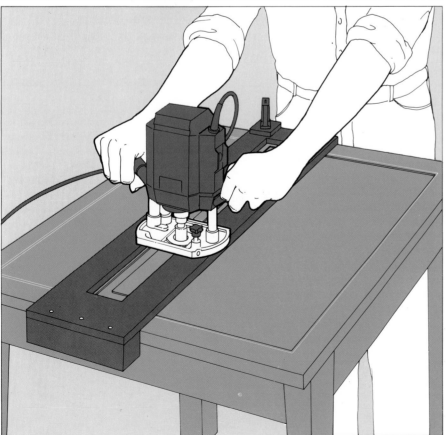

4 **Completing the area.** Undo the cramps and slide the template along the surface so the rectangular cutout overlaps the previous cut by about 2 mm. Pull the batten tight against the workpiece edge, and clamp the template. Rout out the rectangular section exposed within the template, as for the previous one. Continue in this way until the whole area has been removed. Remove the template and square off the corners with a chisel *(page 119)*. Glue and clamp the inlay using the methods shown on page 121.

Picture Credits

The sources for the illustrations in this book are shown below. Credits for the illustrations from left to right are separated by semi-colons, from top to bottom by dashes.

Cover: Fil Hunter. 6: Martin Brigdale. 9, 10: Drawings by Terry Atkinson from Arts & Words. 13: Drawings by Terry Atkinson from Arts & Words (3)—drawing by Oxford Illustrators Ltd. 15: Drawings by Oxford Illustrators Ltd. 16, 17: Drawings by Oxford Illustrators Ltd. 18: Drawings by John Massey—drawing by Oxford Illustrators Ltd. 19–21: Drawings by Oxford Illustrators Ltd. 22: Drawing by Frederic F. Bigio from B-C Graphics. 23: Drawing by Oxford Illustrators Ltd.—drawing by Frederic F. Bigio from B-C Graphics. 24: Drawings by Frederic F. Bigio from B-C Graphics. 25: Drawing by Frederic F. Bigio from B-C Graphics; drawing by Oxford Illustrators Ltd.—drawing by Frederic F. Bigio from B-C Graphics. 26–29: Drawings by Oxford Illustrators Ltd. 30, 31: Drawings by William J. Hennessy Jr. 32: Drawing by William J. Hennessy Jr.—drawing by Oxford Illustrators Ltd. 33: Drawing by Oxford Illustrators Ltd.—drawing by William J. Hennessy Jr. 34: Martin Brigdale. 36: Drawings by Frederic F. Bigio from B-C Graphics. 37: Drawing by Oxford Illus- trators Ltd.—drawing by Frederic F. Bigio from B-C Graphics. 38: Drawing by Frederic F. Bigio from B-C Graphics—drawing by Oxford Illustrators Ltd. 39–41: Drawings by Oxford Illustrators Ltd. 42: Drawing by Frederic F. Bigio from B-C Graphics—drawing by Oxford Illustrators Ltd. 43: Drawing by Frederic F. Bigio from B-C Graphics: drawing by Oxford Illustrators Ltd.—drawing by Frederic F. Bigio from B-C Graphics; drawing by Oxford Illustrators Ltd. 44–49: Drawings by Gerry Gallagher. 50–52; Drawings by William J. Hennessy Jr. 53: Drawing by William J. Hennessy Jr.—drawing by Oxford Illustrators Ltd. 54, 55: Drawings by William J. Hennessy Jr. 56: Drawings by John Massey. 57: Drawings by John Massey—drawing by Oxford Illustrators Ltd.: drawing by John Massey. 58: Drawings by Oxford Illustrators Ltd. 59: Drawings by John Massey. 60: Drawing by Oxford Illustrators Ltd.—drawing by John Massey. 61: Drawing by Oxford Illustrators Ltd.—drawings by John Massey. 62: Drawing by John Massey. 63: Drawings by John Massey— drawing by Oxford Illustrators Ltd. 64, 65: Drawings by Walter Hilmers Jr. from HJ Commercial Art. 66: Drawing by Walter Hilmers Jr. from HJ Commercial Art— drawing by Oxford Illustrators Ltd. 67: Drawings by Oxford Illustrators Ltd. 68: Drawing by Oxford Illustrators Ltd.— drawings by Walter Hilmers Jr. from HJ Commercial Art. 69, 70; Drawings by Oxford Illustrators Ltd. 71: Drawings by Snowden Associates Inc. 72: Drawings by Snowden Associates Inc.—drawing by Oxford Illustrators Ltd. 73: Drawings by Snowden Associates Inc. 74: Martin Brig- dale. 76–81: Drawings by Oxford Illus- trators Ltd. 82: Drawing by Eduino J. Per- eira from Arts & Words—drawing by Oxford Illustrators Ltd. 83: Drawings by Oxford Illustrators Ltd. 84, 85: Drawings by Elsie J. Hennig. 86: Drawing by Elsie J. Hennig—drawing by Oxford Illustrators Ltd. 87–89; Drawings by Elsie J. Hennig. 90–93; Drawings by Frederic F. Bigio from B-C Graphics. 94: Drawings by Oxford Il- lustrators Ltd. 95–99: Drawings by Fre- deric F. Bigio from B-C Graphics. 100–103; Drawings by John Massey. 104–107; Drawings by Oxford Illustrators Ltd. 108: Martin Brigdale. 111–117; Drawings by Frederic F. Bigo from B-C Graphics. 118: Drawing by Oxford Illustrators Ltd. 119: Drawings by William J. Hennessy Jr. 120: Drawings by Oxford Illustrators Ltd. 121: Drawings by William J. Hennessy Jr. 122, 123: Drawings by Oxford Illustrators Ltd.

Acknowledgements

The editors would like to thank the follow- ing: Henry Barrow, The Woodworks, Glen Echo, Maryland, U.S.A.; Juan Bassegoda, President, Amigos de Gaudí, Barcelona, Spain; Bob Blankenship, Moisture Regis- ter Company, North Hollywood, Califor- nia, U.S.A.; Emmett Bright, Rome, Italy; Mario Ceroli, Rome, Italy; Kate Cann, Guildford, Surrey, England; Françoise Charpentier, Curator, Musée de L'Ecole de Nancy, Nancy, France; Ted Chase, Con- cord, California, U.S.A.; Roland Chomel, Grenoble, France; Raylene Decatur, Ren- wick Gallery, Washington, D.C.; Clyde Dorsett, The Pond Gallery, Alexandria, Virginia, U.S.A.; Fendrick Gallery, Wash- ington, D.C.; Allan Fitchett, Albert Con- stantine & Son, Inc., New York; Tim Fraser, Sydney, Australia; Full Circle, Alexandria, Virginia, U.S.A.; Alan Good- win, Kalletal-Talle, West Germany; Doug- las N. Heyman, Fries Beall & Sharp Co., Springfield, Virginia, U.S.A.; Inca Wood- working Machines of Switzerland Ltd., Bletchley, Milton Keynes, Buckingham- shire, England; John Kelsey, Editor, *Fine Woodworking* magazine, Newtown, Con- necticut, U.S.A.; Peter Kramer, Wash- ington, Virginia, U.S.A.; Johannes Kro- gull, Melle, West Germany; Andrejs Legzdins, Stockholm, Sweden; Mike Man- gan, Ken Page, Sears, Roebuck & Co., Chi- cago, Illinois, U.S.A.; John Ott, June Sprigg, Hancock Shaker Village Museum, Pittsfield, Massachusetts, U.S.A.; Robert Petersen, Robert Petersen Associates, Alexandria, Virginia, U.S.A.; Joanne Pol- ster, American Craft Library, The Ameri- can Craft Council, New York; Patricia Ridgeway, Seraph, Washington, D.C.; Giu- seppe Rivadossi, Brescia, Italy; Jerry Sie- gel, Jenks and Sons, Inc., Washington, D.C.; Ole Thrane, L.C.S. Inc., New York; Todd M. Volpe, Jordan-Volpe Gallery, New York; Bill Welcome, Wendell Castle Inc., Scottsdale, New York, U.S.A.

Index/Glossary

Included in this index are definitions of some of the typical terms used in this book. Page references in italics indicate an illustration of the subject mentioned.

Metric Conversion Chart

Approximate equivalents—length

Millimetres to inches		Inches to millimetres	
1	1/32	1/32	1
2	1/16	1/16	2
3	1/8	1/8	3
4	5/32	3/16	5
5	3/16	1/4	6
6	1/4	5/16	8
7	9/32	3/8	10
8	5/16	7/16	11
9	11/32	1/2	13
10 (1cm)	3/8	9/16	14
11	7/16	5/8	16
12	15/32	11/16	17
13	1/2	3/4	19
14	9/16	13/16	21
15	19/32	7/8	22
16	5/8	15/16	24
17	11/16	1	25
18	23/32	2	51
19	3/4	3	76
20	25/32	4	102
25	1	5	127
30	1 3/16	6	152
40	1 9/16	7	178
50	1 31/32	8	203
60	2 3/8	9	229
70	2 3/4	10	254
80	3 5/32	11	279
90	3 9/16	12 (1ft)	305
100	3 15/16	13	330
200	7 7/8	14	356
300	11 13/16	15	381
400	15 3/4	16	406
500	19 11/16	17	432
600	23 5/8	18	457
700	27 9/16	19	483
800	31 1/2	20	508
900	35 7/16	24 (2ft)	610
1000 (1m)	39 3/8		

Metres to feet/inches		Yards to metres	
		1	0.914
2	6' 7"	2	1.83
3	9' 10"	3	2.74
4	13' 1"	4	3.66
5	16' 5"	5	4.57
6	19' 8"	6	5.49
7	23' 0"	7	6.40
8	26' 3"	8	7.32
9	29' 6"	9	8.23
10	32' 10"	10	9.14
20	65' 7"	20	18.29
50	164' 0"	50	45.72
100	328' 1"	100	91.44

Conversion factors

Length

1 millimetre (mm)	= 0.0394 in
1 centimetre (cm)/10 mm	= 0.3937 in
1 metre/100 cm	= 39.37 in/3.281 ft/1.094 yd
1 kilometre (km)/1000 metres	= 1093.6 yd/0.6214 mile
1 inch (in)	= 25.4 mm/2.54 cm
1 foot (ft)/12 in	= 304.8 mm/30.48 cm/0.3048 metre
1 yard (yd)/3 ft	= 914.4 mm/91.44 cm/0.9144 metre
1 mile/1760 yd	= 1609.344 metres/1.609 km

Area

1 square centimetre (sq cm)/ 100 square millimetres (sq mm)	= 0.155 sq in
1 square metre (sq metre)/10,000 sq cm	= 10.764 sq ft/1.196 sq yd
1 are/100 sq metres	= 119.60 sq yd/0.0247 acre
1 hectare (ha)/100 ares	= 2.471 acres/0.00386 sq mile
1 square inch (sq in)	= 645.16 sq mm/6.4516 sq cm
1 square foot (sq ft)/144 sq in	= 929.03 sq cm
1 square yard (sq yd)/9 sq ft	= 8361.3 sq cm/0.8361 sq metre
1 acre/4840 sq yd	= 4046.9 sq metres/0.4047 ha
1 square mile/640 acres	= 259 ha/2.59 sq km

Volume

1 cubic centimetre (cu cm)/ 1000 cubic millimetres (cu mm)	= 0.0610 cu in
1 cubic decimetre (cu dm)/1000 cu cm	= 61.024 cu in/0.0353 cu ft
1 cubic metre/1000 cu dm	= 35.3147 cu ft/1.308 cu yd
1 cu cm	= 1 millilitre (ml)
1 cu dm	= 1 litre see **Capacity**
1 cubic inch (cu in)	= 16.3871 cu cm
1 cubic foot (cu ft)/1728 cu in	= 28,316.8 cu cm/0·0283 cu metre
1 cubic yard (cu yd)/27 cu ft	= 0.7646 cu metre

Capacity

1 litre	= 1.7598 pt/0.8799 qt/0.22 gal
1 pint (pt)	= 0.568 litre
1 quart (qt)	= 1.137 litres
1 gallon (gal)	= 4.546 litres

Weight

1 gram (g)	= 0.035 oz
1 kilogram (kg)/1000 g	= 2.20 lb/35.2 oz
1 tonne/1000 kg	= 2204.6 lb/0.9842 ton
1 ounce (oz)	= 28.35 g
1 pound (lb)	= 0.4536 kg
1 ton	= 1016 kg

Pressure

1 gram per square metre (g/metre^2)	= 0.0295 oz/sq yd
1 gram per square centimetre (g/cm^2)	= 0.228 oz/sq in
1 kilogram per square centimetre (kg/cm^2)	= 14.223 lb/sq in
1 kilogram per square metre (kg/metre^2)	= 0.205 lb/sq ft
1 pound per square foot (lb/ft^2)	= 4.882 kg/metre^2
1 pound per square inch (lb/in^2)	= 703.07 kg/metre^2
1 ounce per square yard (oz/yd^2)	= 33.91 g/metre^2
1 ounce per square foot (oz/ft^2)	= 305.15 g/metre^2

Temperature

To convert °F to °C, subtract 32, then divide by 9 and multiply by 5

To convert °C to °F, divide by 5 and multiply by 9, then add 32

Phototypeset by Tradespools Limited, Frome, Somerset
Colour reproduction by Grafascan Limited, Dublin, Ireland
Printed and bound by Artes Gráficas, Toledo, SA, Spain

D. L. TO:1164 -1986